Dr. Hall answers every woman's questions . . .

What are the most common physical symptoms of pregnancy?

What are the pros and cons of natural childbirth?

Should you push your husband into attending the delivery?

What is a husband expected to do during labor?

What are the dangers of medication during labor?

When is the induction of labor necessary?

How soon after delivery should nursing begin?

What are the common problems encountered in taking the baby home?

What happens during the first postpartum visit to the doctor?

And much, much more!

NINE MONTHS' READING

"Provides the information necessary to minimize a woman's concern about pregnancy, labor and delivery. This edition will make excellent reading for both the prospective mother and father. In a lucid manner, Dr. Hall has written an excellent book that should be of great assistance to pregnant women."

 —Theodore M. King, M.D., Ph.D.
  Director of Gynecology and Obstetrics
  The John Hopkins University Medical School

Bantam Books of Related Interest
Ask your bookseller for the books you have missed

THE BABY CHECKUP BOOK: A PARENT'S GUIDE TO
  WELL BABY CARE by Sheila Hillman
THE BETTER HOMES & GARDENS NEW BABY BOOK
CHILD'S BODY from The Diagram Group
THE COMPLETE BOOK OF BREASTFEEDING by
  Marvin S. Eiger, M.D. & Sally Wendkos Olds
FEED ME! I'M YOURS by Vicki Lansky
THE FIRST TWELVE MONTHS OF LIFE,
  Frank Caplan, editor
INFANT MASSAGE by Vimala Schneider
NO-NONSENSE NUTRITION FOR YOUR BABY'S FIRST
  YEAR by Joanne Heslin, Annette B. Natow
  and Barbara C. Raven
THE SECOND TWELVE MONTHS OF LIFE,
  Frank Caplan, editor
SIGH OF RELIEF; THE FIRST AID HANDBOOK FOR
  CHILDHOOD EMERGENCIES by Martin Green
THE TAMING OF THE C.A.N.D.Y. MONSTER by
  Vicki Lansky

QUANTITY PURCHASES

Companies, professional groups, churches, clubs and other
organizations may qualify for special terms when ordering
24 or more copies of this title. For information, contact the
Direct Response Department, Bantam Books, 666 Fifth
Avenue, New York, N.Y. 10103. Phone (212) 765-6500.

NINE MONTHS' READING

A Medical Guide
for Pregnant Women

THIRD REVISED EDITION

Robert E. Hall, M.D.

Illustrated by Robert Demarest

BANTAM BOOKS
TORONTO · NEW YORK · LONDON · SYDNEY

NINE MONTHS' READING:
A MEDICAL GUIDE FOR PREGNANT WOMEN

*A Bantam Book / published by arrangement with
Doubleday & Company, Inc.*

PRINTING HISTORY

*Original Doubleday edition published September 1960
Revised Doubleday edition published September 1963*
2nd printing ...... March 1964   3rd printing ...... January 1965
*New Revised Doubleday edition published October 1972
Doubleday fourth edition published November 1982*

*Bantam edition / May 1965
8 printings through May 1972
Revised Bantam edition / October 1973*

2nd printing .... April 1974	8th printing .... March 1978
3rd printing .... October 1974	9th printing ..... November 1978
4th printing .... May 1975	10th printing .... July 1979
5th printing .... March 1976	11th printing .... December 1979
6th printing .... April 1977	12th printing .... July 1980
7th printing .... August 1977	13th printing .....September 1981

Bantam third edition / September 1983

All rights reserved.
Copyright © 1960, 1963, 1972, 1983 by Robert E. Hall.
Cover art copyright © 1983 by Bantam Books, Inc.
*This book may not be reproduced in whole or in part, by
mimeograph or any other means, without permission.*
*For information address: Doubleday & Co., Inc.,
245 Park Avenue, New York, N.Y. 10167.*

ISBN 0-553-23122-7

Published simultaneously in the United States and Canada

Bantam Books are published by Bantam Books, Inc. Its trademark, consisting
of the words "Bantam Books" and the portrayal of a rooster, is Registered
in U.S. Patent and Trademark Office and in other countries. Marca Registrada.
Bantam Books, Inc., 666 Fifth Avenue, New York, New York 10103.

PRINTED IN THE UNITED STATES OF AMERICA

O   0 9 8 7 6 5 4 3 2 1

To my good friends and colleagues,
Dr. Susan W. Williamson
and
Dr. Richard S. Banfield, Jr.

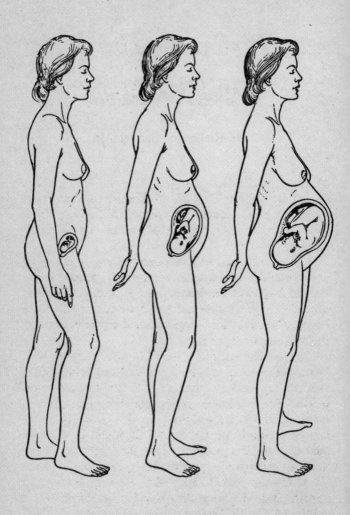

THREE STAGES OF PREGNANCY. The mother is depicted in approximately the third, sixth, and ninth months of pregnancy.

Preface to Third Revised Edition

The basic mechanisms of making love and having babies do not change. But the field of obstetrics becomes more scientific and complicated every year. Unbelievable progress has been made since the first edition of *Nine Months' Reading*.

In 1959, when this book was first written, there was no way to prevent Rh disease of the newborn, genetic abnormalities could not be detected in the fetus, the vaccine against German measles had not been discovered. Panty hose had not even been invented. And a private room in the hospital cost $15 to $20 a day.

Changes have occurred in my life too. Recently, after twenty-five years of delivering babies (and loving it), I switched my field to psychiatry. While specializing in women's emotional problems and maintaining my interest in obstetrics, I did not feel that I could do justice to updating this book without the help of those still in the forefront of obstetrical progress. I have been fortunate in my choice of colleagues to provide this assistance: Dr. Susan W. Williamson and Dr. Richard S. Banfield, Jr., both of whom worked with me at the Columbia-Presbyterian Medical Center. Dr. Williamson has remained on the Medical Center staff for thirty-plus years and Dr. Banfield has established an active obstetrical practice in Stamford, Connecticut. Through many hours of consultation they have shared their expertise with me. It is with pride and pleasure that I have dedicated this edition of *Nine Months' Reading* to them.

For any pregnancy guide to be of value it must be updated often. The present revision has been comprehensive. It should, I hope, provide up-to-date answers to most of your questions—until new information is available, when new editions will be written.

April 1982

R.E.H.

Contents

Preface to Third Revised Edition   vii

Illustrations   xi

Introduction   xiii

1 *The Patient and Her Doctor* / American   1
   Obstetrics Today; Selecting a Doctor; Selecting a
   Hospital; Doctors' Partnerships; Doctors' Fees;
   Hospital Rates; The First Office Visit; Subsequent
   Visits; Between Visits

2 *Development of the Fetus* / Female Anatomy;   16
   Ovulation and Menstruation; Fertilization;
   Migration of the Ovum; The Fetus, Placenta,
   and Membranes; Activities of the Fetus; The Size
   of the Fetus

3 *Symptoms and Sensations* / Morning Sickness;   28
   Lethargy; Frequency of Urination; Swelling and
   Tenderness of the Breasts; Abdominal Swelling;
   Flatulence; Heartburn; Quickening; Skin
   Pigmentation; Leg Cramps; Varicose Veins;
   Hemorrhoids; Constipation; Backache; Groin
   Pains; Striae; Nosebleeds; Angiomas; Faintness
   and Dizziness; Insomnia; Moodiness; Shortness
   of Breath; Vaginal Discharge; Swollen Ankles;
   Husbands' Symptoms

4 *Rules and Regulations* / Diet; Cigarettes,   39
   Alcohol, and Drugs; Douching, Intercourse, and
   Tub Baths; Work; Rest; Exercise; Travel;
   Moving and Painting; Clothes; Teeth; Breast and

Skin Care; Vaccinations; Sex of the Baby; The
Father and the Grandmother; Packing a Bag

5 *Complications of Pregnancy* / Miscarriages;   58
Ectopic Pregnancies; Multiple Pregnancies;
German Measles; The Hazards of X-ray
and Ultrasound; Malformation of the Baby;
Death of the Fetus; The Rh Factor; Toxemia of
Pregnancy; Maternal Diseases; Maternal Deaths;
Surgery During Pregnancy; Induced Abortion;
Sterilization

6 *Normal Labor and Delivery* / The Duration of   84
Pregnancy; Premonitory Sensations; Causes of
the Onset of Labor; The Physiology of Labor;
Subjective Sensations of Labor; Labor-room
Routine; Medication During Labor; Anesthesia;
The Delivery; The Episiotomy; The Induction
of Labor; Natural Childbirth; Prepared Childbirth

7 *Abnormal Labor and Delivery* / Premature   116
Rupture of the Membranes; Premature Labor;
Slow Labor; Dry Labor; Cephalopelvic
Disproportion; Cesarean Sections; Placenta Previa;
Premature Separation of the Placenta; Breech
Presentation

8 *Motherhood in the Hospital* / The Recovery   128
Room; Minor Annoyances; Serious Complications;
Rooming-in; Breast Feeding; Bottle Feeding;
The Newborn Baby; Hospital Routines;
Preparation for Going Home

9 *Motherhood at Home* / The First Day; Help;   154
Activities; Diet; Menstruation; Complications;
Baby Care; The Postpartum Visit

Glossary of Obstetrical Terms   165

Index   173

Illustrations

1 THREE STAGES OF PREGNANCY

2 FEMALE ANATOMY 17

3 FERTILIZATION OF THE EGG 20

4 THE DETERMINATION OF SEX 21

5 OVULATION TO IMPLANTATION 22

6 THE GROWING FETUS 26

7 WEIGHT GAIN 41

8 ECTOPIC PREGNANCY 62

9 AMNIOCENTESIS 69

10 STERILIZATION 82

11 LABOR 88–89

12 FETAL MONITORING 97

13 REGIONAL ANESTHESIA 102

14 THE DELIVERY ROOM 104

15 FORCEPS DELIVERY 107

16 BREECH PRESENTATION 126

17 THE NURSING MOTHER 135

18 HELP AT HOME 155

ABOUT THE AUTHOR

ROBERT E. HALL, M.D., has practiced obstetrics and gynecology at Columbia-Presbyterian Medical Center in New York City. After 25 years of obstetrics, he recently switched his speciality to psychiatry but has kept in touch with his former field, and for this new edition of NINE MONTHS' READING he has relied heavily on consultation with obstetrical colleagues for the latest medical information.

ROBERT DEMAREST, the artist, is well known for his work in the fields of medical books and medical advertising.

Introduction

Modern women want to know the why and wherefore of everything. As they should. When pregnant, they are not satisfied with a simple explanation of the birth process. They want to know about German measles, X-rays, the Rh factor, birth defects, anesthesia, rooming-in, breast feeding, and a multitude of other factors that are involved in the pregnancy process. The purpose of this book is to satisfy, insofar as possible, this healthy intellectual curiosity.

This is not a textbook dealing with obstetrical technicalities; nor is it a fairy tale proposing that pregnancy is to be lightly regarded. I have taken a middle road in the approach and scope of the book, attempting to be comprehensive but not pedantic, reassuring but not platitudinous. I have not, however, taken the middle road on specific issues such as natural childbirth and breast feeding. Although I have tried to present both sides of these more controversial subjects, my own personal views are readily apparent. Since my views are the product, I hope, more of my training and experience than of innate prejudice on my part, I feel that it is preferable to record them for your appraisal rather than to avoid taking a stand. Inevitably it is you who must decide whether to try natural childbirth and breast feeding. I feel that you will be better prepared to make these decisions if you can weigh the pros, the cons, and as much advice as you can get from those of us who deal with these matters every day.

I have made the basic assumption that the reader of this

book has a minimum of obstetrical knowledge and a maximum of curiosity about pregnancy, labor, delivery, and the early stage of motherhood. It was unavoidable that a smattering of obstetrical terms be used; a glossary at the end of the book will serve to define these terms for those of you who are unfamiliar with them. It is my hope that this book will be read by both the expectant mother and the expectant father. Ideally, it should be read once from beginning to end and then used as a source of reference if and when individual questions arise.

From a glance at the Contents you might infer that undue emphasis is placed on the abnormal or disagreeable aspects of pregnancy. Actually an attempt is made throughout the text to stress the normality of the pregnant state, but the normal warrants less amplification than the abnormal. After all, one does not need to refer to a book often if all is going well. While many of you will experience none of the obstetrical problems discussed here, it might be reassuring to those of you who do develop unexpected symptoms to have already learned which of them are obstetrically significant and what they portend.

It is, I am sure, superfluous to point out that this book is meant to supplement rather than to supplant the guidance which you will receive from your own obstetrician. I have not studded the text with reminders to this effect, for it must be obvious that if you are hemorrhaging or hurting, for example, you should consult your doctor, not a book. One of the defects inherent in the written word is that it must generalize; only your obstetrician knows what is best for you as an individual. I hope nevertheless that this book will provide a background of useful information for you, a background upon which your own doctor can draw the details best suited to your case.

ROBERT E. HALL, M.D.

1

The Patient and Her Doctor

By far the majority of babies born in the history of this world were born without benefit of any formal obstetrical care. Indeed there are many millions of human beings on our globe today who have no access to medical care of any sort. And in many civilized countries—most of Europe, for example—the bulk of obstetrics is performed by mid-wives.

AMERICAN OBSTETRICS TODAY

Why then do most American women seek the services of an obstetrician? Why are 95 percent of the deliveries in the United States performed in hospitals, almost all of them by doctors? The simplest answer lies in the fact that this type of care produces the lowest maternal and infant death rates. To illustrate: in 1940, when only about half of the deliveries in this country took place in hospitals, the maternal mortality was 40 times what it is today. And in the past thirty years the neonatal death rate (the rate of infant death during the first week after delivery) has been cut in half, largely by improvements in the hospital care of premature babies.

These are crude but meaningful measures of the quality of obstetrical care. Healthy women no longer die from pregnancy and childbirth, and healthy infants have a life expectancy of more than seventy years. This accomplishment has been achieved through greater knowledge, better facilities, improved equipment, and increased specialization.

The Obstetrician's Role. Mortality statistics are not the only answer by any means. If you never go to a doctor during your pregnancy and if you let your next-door neighbor deliver your baby, the chances are that both you and your baby will survive the experience. But you may bleed a good deal, you may become infected, and you may develop any one of a great many complications, some of which you may not discover until years later; and the baby is especially prone to problems during the first few hours after birth. The modern obstetrician is trained and the modern hospital is equipped to prevent these complications in most instances, and to treat them promptly and properly when they occur. In actual practice it is difficult for a patient to assess the role of her obstetrician, for so much of his work is preventative; it is hard to appreciate being spared a complication if you are unaware of even the threat of its existence. Much of the remainder of your doctor's function is practically indefinable, for you will find that he or she becomes a source of confidence and trust as well as information and guidance.

The Midwife's Role. In certain areas of the country, notably California and Connecticut, midwives are assuming a more active role in prenatal care and delivery. Their practice is limited to normal pregnancies, usually with backup coverage by an obstetrician in case complications arise. There are two kinds: "certified midwives," usually nurses, who have undergone special training and been certified by a board; and "lay midwives," who have not necessarily had any formal training. Certified midwives often work with doctors in office and hospital settings; lay midwives perform home deliveries. In my opinion a well-trained midwife is a valuable adjunct to the obstetrical scene and I assume that she will play an increasingly active role in years to come. Home deliveries, on the other hand, seem too risky to recommend.

SELECTING A DOCTOR

When it comes to the matter of choosing an obstetrician, it is difficult to give advice which will be equally appropriate in little hamlets, medium-sized towns, and big cities. The usual method, of course, is to seek the recommendation of one's friends and family, much as one does in finding a good electrician or plumber. But it is obviously more important to find a skilled doctor, for a woman is naturally more concerned about her body than about her radio or her bathtub.

The Doctor's Qualifications. There are many clues by which one can measure the merits of one's prospective obstetrician. Among these are his training, his experience, his specialty rating, his hospital affiliations, and his patients' regard for him.* Of these several yardsticks, probably the most important is the first, his training. If a doctor has been thoroughly trained in his specialty, by attending a first-rate medical school and then pursuing a residency at a first-rate hospital, there is little chance of his not being sufficiently capable to handle whatever situations arise within his field. If he has also been certified by his specialty board and is practicing at the best hospital in your community, then you have all the evidence you need of his

* Could we assume, please, from here on that whenever I refer to a doctor as "he" I truly mean "he or she"? It would be frightfully awkward to write "his or her training, his or her experience, his or her specialty rating," et cetera. Believe me, I have the highest regard for female physicians and I regret the fact that there is no gender-free pronoun. I shall try to compensate for this unintentional bias by referring to the baby, later on, as "she" and "her."

capabilities. There are probably several physicians in your community who fulfill all of these qualifications. In the United States there are more than 22,000 doctors who have been certified by the American Board of Obstetrics and Gynecology, and perhaps 5,000 others who limit their practice to obstetrics and gynecology.

Doctors' Recommendations. As for how you are going to get this sort of information about an obstetrician, the best way is simply to ask any other respected physician in your area. Tell him you want the names of the best obstetricians in town and don't be embarrassed to inquire about their professional pedigrees. Directories which contain a fund of detailed information about every specialist in the country are available to the entire medical profession. The chances are that your own family doctor knows the names of several qualified obstetricians; if not, he can obtain this knowledge through such a directory.

Specialist or G.P. If the above remarks seem to indicate that, generally speaking, I feel that a pregnant woman will get better obstetrical care from a specialist (one whose entire training and practice have been devoted to obstetrics and gynecology), this is indeed true. But this is not meant to imply for one second that there are not thousands of other doctors who are capable of rendering good obstetrical care. Their training may have been less formal and less extensive, but this is where the element of experience becomes important, for many general practitioners have delivered so many thousands of babies that they have achieved considerable obstetrical skill. They may not be able to perform some of the more intricate types of delivery, but in the event that complications arise they usually can enlist the services of a specialist who practices at the same hospital. There is no shortage of good obstetricians in America today.

The Pediatrician. It is important to select a pediatrician some time before the baby comes. He may want to see you before the delivery in order to discuss upcoming events. He will probably want to examine the baby in the hospital (in fact many hospitals insist on this) and he will want to see the baby soon after you go home. If you don't know a good pediatrician in your neighborhood, ask your obstetrician to recommend one.

SELECTING A HOSPITAL

The problem of choosing a hospital is inseparable from that of choosing a doctor; by and large the solution of one will lead to the solution of the other. The better doctors are almost invariably given privileges to practice at the better hospitals, and so if you are fortunate enough to know a good obstetrician he will undoubtedly take you to a good hospital. Conversely, if you don't know a good doctor, one of the best ways to find one is to call the best hospital in town and ask for the recommendation of a doctor on its staff.

As far as obstetrics is concerned, the choice of doctor is usually more important than the choice of hospital, for a competent obstetrician will rarely need equipment more elaborate than that found in any one of the more than 7,000 hospitals in the country which have been approved by the American Medical Association. The advantages of the larger medical centers include their better laboratory facilities, diagnostic equipment, anesthesia departments, and blood banks, and the ready availability of first-rate consultants in every branch of medicine; but these advantages are essential to the management of only the more complicated obstetrical problems.

Alternate Birth Centers. In response to public demand for a less clinical setting for the labor and delivery process, "alternate birth centers" have been created. In contrast to the Spartan hospital surroundings of the conventional labor and delivery rooms, these facilities offer an atmosphere which simulates that of your home. They may be free-standing—i.e., physically separate from a hospital—in which case the deliveries are performed by midwives. Or they may be located within the confines of a hospital, where the delivery may be performed by a midwife or a physician and complications can be handled down the hall. Customarily the postpartum stay in these centers is shorter (one or two days) than in the ordinary hospital setting. If you are interested in this kind of ambience, ask your doctor if it is available at the hospital where he works.

DOCTORS' PARTNERSHIPS

Another matter worth mentioning is the many ways in which obstetricians manage to cover their practices 365 days out of every year. Every patient concedes her obstetrician's right to an occasional vacation and weekend away from the phone, but no patient wants her obstetrician to be unavailable when she needs him. Unfortunately this normal desire is sometimes thwarted by this realistic concession.

Most obstetricians, when they go "off call" for a weekend or a month, leave their patients in the hands of a trusted colleague. In order for you to meet this second doctor (and vice versa), you may be asked to see him in his office several times before your delivery, especially in the event of a planned vacation. Other obstetricians arrange their vacations a year in advance and refuse to take on new patients whose deliveries will probably occur during that month.

Because of the tremendous sacrifice in personal freedom which accrues to a busy obstetrician, an increasing number of them have formed partnerships of various kinds. To be responsible for the care and delivery of 300, 200, or even 100 women a year is, as you might imagine, a pretty strenuous undertaking for one physician. And so Dr. X may alternate weekends and vacations with Dr. Y. If you are Dr. X's patient, you may never meet Dr. Y unless you happen to need him during one of his weekends on call. Or you may see Dr. X and Dr. Y, and sometimes even a third doctor,

Dr. Z, on alternate visits and you may not know until you actually go into labor which doctor is going to deliver your baby. There are all sorts of arrangements, most of them following these rough lines, and different women react differently to them; but as these types of group medicine have become more widely known they have become more widely accepted. In a sense a patient might rightfully resent not having the individual attention of one doctor, whose availability she can count upon at all times, but the most reassuring fact behind any such partnership arrangement is that the abilities of each doctor are invariably similar to those of his partners or otherwise they would not choose to practice together.

DOCTORS' FEES

Average Fees. It is impossible to generalize on this tender subject, for fees vary somewhat from patient to patient, from doctor to doctor, and from community to community. Most obstetricians charge a flat rate for their service, which includes antepartum† care, labor, delivery, hospital care, and at least one postpartum visit. Ask the doctor on your first visit not only what his fee will be but also what it covers. There are, of course, a few unpredictable extras for which legitimate additional charges are sometimes made—such as the performance of a cesarean section or circumcision—but routine procedures such as forceps deliveries and episiotomies are almost invariably covered.

In the bigger cities the going rate for this nine-month care by a specialist is $1,000 to $1,500. In less populated areas the fee is generally less, largely because the doctor's malpractice premiums are less. In case you haven't heard, the annual malpractice premium for an obstetrician in some of the larger cities in 1982 was $35,000—and going up yearly.

† Medical terms that may be new to you are defined in the Glossary at the end of this book.

What You're Buying. When you pay your obstetrician you are buying many intangibles: his training, his experience, his availability, his patience, his confidence, his knowledge, and his time. In terms of his actual service to you, he will probably see you in his office twelve times before the delivery, spend six hours in the labor room suite with you, visit you four times in the hospital and once again in his office six weeks later. And this calculation does not include the phone calls, the lost sleep, the delayed meals, and the time involved in getting to and from the hospital. You may see the doctor only five times and your labor may take only two hours, while your neighbor may see him twenty times and be in labor for two days; it wouldn't be fair to charge her a bigger fee, any more than it would be fair to charge a fat man more for his suits.

Health Insurance. Most people have health insurance, which helps to defray the hospital's and doctor's charges. In my opinion, anyone who does not have health insurance these days is either very wealthy or irresponsible. Some insurance companies, particularly those covering the employees of large corporations, pay all of the doctor and hospital bills. Others, such as Blue Cross and Blue Shield, may pay as much as 80 percent, depending on the type of policy. Whatever your coverage, make sure that it is in order well in advance of a planned pregnancy and check specifically on its maternity benefits.

Other Expenses. Most obstetricians do not charge additionally for routine laboratory tests. Expect to pay extra, though, for unusual procedures such as amniocentesis (about $250 to $300). Some doctors charge more for cesarean sections; you should ask about this in advance and check on how it is covered by your insurance policy. If a consultant is called in (e.g., to help decide whether a cesarean is necessary), he will submit a bill too. The anesthesiologist will submit a bill (sometimes calculated by the hour) which may not be covered by insurance. You should discuss fees with your pediatrician too; he may charge by the visit or by the year. And, finally, bear in mind that all of these costs are going up—just like the cost of your groceries.

HOSPITAL RATES

Average Rates. Hospital charges also vary somewhat from city to city, within the same city, and within the same hospital. Few hospitals actually try to make a profit; in fact it is almost impossible nowadays for a private hospital to operate in the black. Every year hospital rates go up as hospitals have to buy more modern equipment and pay more for drugs, labor, and materials.

In the larger cities a semiprivate room may cost $150 or more a day; private accommodations may start at $200. In addition there will be a charge of perhaps $100 a day for the nursery, $300 for the use of the delivery room, and $50 for medicines and lab tests. All of these charges are apt to be lower in the suburbs and small towns. With semiprivate care you may have one to five roommates. With a private room you have the luxury of privacy, a separate bathroom, and sometimes fancier food and more liberal visiting hours. A room by yourself is more restful; any desire for companionship can be satisfied by visiting the other new mothers down the hall.

Ward Accommodations. Most patients who have health insurance can afford to have their own doctors; for those who cannot afford private care, many hospitals provide ward obstetrical service, which is covered by Medicaid or other insurance carriers. In addition, in the larger cities there are municipal hospitals which provide free care to those who cannot afford to pay. There is no excuse for an American woman's not having complete medical attention throughout her pregnancy.

Ward care differs from private care in that it is usually rendered by the interns and residents who are one to five years out of medical school and in the process of learning obstetrics. Their work is done under the supervision of the attending physicians and therefore it is usually on a par with the private work at the same hospital. The principal sacrifices made by a ward patient are, in varying degrees, the elements of privacy and individual attention.

THE FIRST OFFICE VISIT

When to Go. Having suspected that you are pregnant and having selected a prospective obstetrician, how soon should you make your first appointment? The answer to this will vary a little from patient to patient. Patients with medical problems, such as diabetes, and patients who have had previous miscarriages should seek attention as soon as they have missed their first menstrual period; otherwise it is generally advisable to wait another month. If you see your doctor sooner it may be impossible for him to make a definite diagnosis of pregnancy without taking a pregnancy test, which is usually not otherwise necessary; if you wait until later you may find yourself without a doctor when an early complication develops.

Pregnancy tests in the doctor's office are usually done from a blood sample and the results are available in a few hours. Or you may buy a kit in the drugstore for about $10 and test your urine.

What to Expect. This first visit to your obstetrician is a supremely important occasion at which you will learn a great deal about your doctor and yourself and he in turn will learn a great deal about you. There is no reason it should be any more frightening than the experience of making any other new acquaintance. The first visit usually entails a complete medical history and physical examination and certain laboratory tests. Your doctor will ask pertinent questions about your previous health, your menstrual periods, your previous pregnancies, and many other subjects, the answers to which will help him to supervise your pregnancy intelligently.

The physical examination at the initial visit will cover everything from head to toe. From this the doctor will learn your weight, your blood pressure, the condition of your teeth, the sound of your heart, the size of your liver, the shape of your pelvis, the age of your pregnancy, and much more. The pelvic examination will seem a little different from those you might have had before, for from it your doctor must learn not only whether or not you have any gynecological abnormality, but also whether your pregnancy seems normal and whether your pelvis seems adequate in size and contour to permit the easy vaginal delivery of an average-sized infant. Most women are somewhat embarrassed by pelvic examinations; doctors are aware of this and take it into consideration. The more you relax, however, the easier and quicker this procedure will be. There is usually no reason to repeat the pelvic examination until the very end of pregnancy.

A complete urinalysis, blood count, and Pap smear are usually performed at this first visit, and blood will be taken from your arm to determine your hemoglobin level, blood group, Rh factor, Wassermann reaction, and your immunity to rubella. These tests serve the purpose of enabling your doctor to foresee and, when possible, to prevent or treat anemia, erythroblastosis, syphilis, and other complications. Some obstetricians defer some or all of these investigations until the second visit, but if they haven't been performed by then it would behoove you to find out why. A skin test should be done to detect tuberculosis and, if it is positive, a chest X-ray will be performed when you get to the seventh month. If there is any suggestion of heart trouble an electrocardiogram may be ordered.

Many doctors prescribe prenatal capsules to their patients at the first visit; these capsules contain vitamins, iron, calcium, and sometimes fluoride, which are often necessary supplements to a pregnant woman's diet. And if there are any specific complaints, such as excessive nausea, he may prescribe medication for them too.

Questions to Ask. This visit also gives the patient an opportunity to learn more about her obstetrician and to ask his views on any particular problems or questions she might have. If you are especially interested in natural childbirth (see Chapter 6), breast feeding (see Chapter 8), or rooming-in (see Chapter 8), this is a good time to ask about them; and if you have any particular fears in connection with pregnancy, labor, or delivery, now is the time to voice them. Your doctor will probably also give you some dietary instructions and perhaps some general information about what you should or should not do while pregnant. And he will explain how and where to reach him and who may take his place in the event that he is unavailable when you need him. This is also the best time to discuss the doctor's fee, hospital charges, insurance payments, and like matters.

Genetic Counseling. During this interview the doctor will want to explore the unpleasant subject of birth defects in order to determine whether your pregnancy poses any special genetic risk. He will want to know if there is a history, in your family or the father's, of Tay-Sachs disease (most common in Jews), sickle cell anemia (only in blacks), Cooley's anemia (in Greeks, Italians, and Iranians), hemophilia (only in males), Down's syndrome (mongolism), or other hereditary diseases. If there is such a history or in any case if you are over thirty-five (when the incidence of Down's syndrome rises drastically) you should consider having an amniocentesis in order to determine whether your fetus is affected. This test (see Chapter 5) is performed after the fifteenth week. There is also a blood test which may be performed on Jewish couples to determine whether Tay-Sachs disease may develop in the fetus.

SUBSEQUENT VISITS

The time intervals between your subsequent visits will be decided by your doctor on an individual basis but, generally speaking, the average obstetrical patient is seen monthly through the seventh month, every two weeks during the eighth month, and then every week until delivery. Thus during a typical pregnancy the patient is seen about a dozen times. These later visits are usually briefer than the initial one for rather obvious reasons. If you have had any symptoms since the previous visit, this is the time to discuss them; and if you have any questions about whether you should travel, when you should stop working, or anything else, this is the time to ask them. Your doctor expects questions and it is part of his job to answer them. He will then check your weight, blood pressure, the size of your baby, its position and its heartbeat (if it is detectable yet), and note any unusual developments such as swollen ankles. If he discovers anything potentially troublesome he will probably prescribe appropriate remedies or advise you to take certain precautions. If nothing seems amiss and you have no particular problems these visits may take only five or ten minutes. Sometimes the routine tests and examinations are performed by midwives or physicians' assistants (P.A.s) who work with the doctor.

The Family. If you want to take your husband, children, or mother to these visits, ask your doctor how he feels about this. Most obstetricians these days welcome their participation, feeling that pregnancy is a family experience which should be shared by all family members.

The Fetal Heartbeat. The fetal heartbeat can now be detected with the Doptone, an instrument using high-frequency ultrasound, sometimes as early as ten and a half weeks from the last menstrual period. Through the stethoscope it cannot usually be heard until the fifth or even the seventh month. The time of its first detection varies with the thickness of the patient's abdominal wall, the amount of amniotic fluid (the water surrounding the fetus), and the position of the baby. There is no cause for alarm if the heartbeat cannot be heard, as long as you can feel the baby move.

Preparation for Nursing. Ideally you should decide whether you are going to nurse your baby well in advance of her arrival, for if your nipples are unduly tender they can be toughened or, if inverted, they can be brought out by simple daily manipulations prescribed by your physician.

Pelvic Examinations. Toward the end of your pregnancy more time will be devoted to the attempt to predict how big your baby will be and how soon it will come. Pelvic examinations may be performed in order to determine how far the fetus has descended and how much, if at all, your cervix has dilated. Estimates of fetal weights and delivery dates are, at best, approximate.

BETWEEN VISITS

Danger Signs. If you develop some new problem between appointments with your doctor, your doctor will expect you to call him. But, as you know, he doesn't expect to be called for every trivial complaint, so it might be worthwhile here to enumerate some of the danger signs which he wants to know about. These are the most important ones: (1) Vaginal bleeding. (2) Leakage of clear fluid from the vagina. (3) Abdominal pain of any kind. (4) Persistent headaches. (5) Puffiness or swelling, if more than slight, of the hands, feet, or face. (6) Any significant illness characterized by fever, rash, or diarrhea.

House Calls. If your problem is of an obstetrical nature your doctor may want to see you in his office or in the hospital or he may tell you what to do at home. If it is of a general medical nature which can't be handled over the phone, he may want to see you in his office or at the hospital, or he may want you to be seen by your family doctor. Generally speaking, obstetricians make very few house calls, since there is absolutely nothing which can be done in the home for most obstetrical problems, such as bleeding, and a house call might in such an instance mean the waste of valuable time, both his and yours.

Telephone Technique. When you do decide to call your

obstetrician, you should be prepared to do so in an intelligent manner. In the first place, if it is humanly possible *place the call yourself*. Neither your husband nor your mother can give as accurate a description of your symptoms as you can. Second, be prepared to give a reasonable estimate of the quantity and quality of what is going on—how much you're bleeding, hurting, or leaking. Third, have a pad and pencil handy in case the doctor gives you some instructions. And, finally, jot down the name and telephone number of your local druggist, in case the doctor wants to prescribe some medicine for you.

If the doctor is not in his office when you call, his secretary will look for him and ask him to call you back; in the meantime, don't tie up the wire by calling other people. If the matter is extremely urgent (i.e., if you are hemorrhaging or having labor pains every few minutes) and your call is not returned within a reasonable length of time, it is probably best for you to go to the hospital while they continue to look for him. Usually an obstetrician is easy to find, for he lets his answering service know where he is every minute of the day and he probably wears an electronic beeper on his belt, so that he can be reached immediately, even on the golf course or at the theater.

2

Development of the Fetus

The increasing prevalence of sex education courses notwithstanding, most American adults do not fully understand the mechanism whereby a pregnancy evolves and develops. It is a fascinating story. Let me tell it to you.

FEMALE ANATOMY

With rare exceptions, every woman is endowed with a vagina, a uterus (or womb), two fallopian tubes, and two ovaries. The lower part of the uterus is called the cervix (sometimes referred to as the neck of the womb, for *cervix* is Latin for neck). The cervix is composed mainly of tough elastic tissue and it contains a tiny canal through which the vagina is connected with the cavity of the uterus. The fallopian tubes, in turn, open at one end into the uterine cavity and at the other end directly into the abdomen. Thus in the female there is a direct pathway from the outside world by way of the vagina, the cervix, the uterus, and the tubes to the abdominal cavity itself. In their natural state, of course, all of these organs, including the vagina, are collapsed. Air and water cannot enter the vagina and ascend into the uterus, for the cervical canal is ordinarily

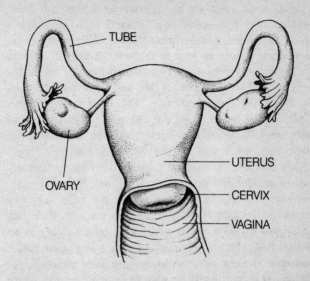

TUBE

UTERUS

OVARY

CERVIX

VAGINA

FEMALE ANATOMY. Part of the vaginal wall is cut away to show the cervix.

filled with a plug of impermeable mucus. But this uninterrupted chain of canals and cavities can, of course, be traversed by the spermatozoa.

OVULATION AND MENSTRUATION

The ovaries, which are located near the abdominal openings of the tubes, have two very important functions: to manufacture the eggs and to produce the female hormones. The ovaries of every female infant at birth contain thousands of tiny individual cells, the "primordial germ cells," some of which are destined to become ova, or eggs, which may or may not become fertilized. Every month, during the reproductive years of a woman (the years that she menstruates), several of these primordial ova, which have lain dormant in her ovaries since she was born, develop into fertilizable eggs, around each of which a small fluid-filled follicle forms. These follicles reach the size of about half an inch in diameter and then, approximately halfway between two menstrual periods, one of the eggs bursts through the paper-thin wall of its follicle and escapes into the abdominal cavity. This would seem a rather foolish thing for it to do, for the egg, which consists of only one cell and is just barely visible to the naked eye, then finds itself free in the relatively enormous space which contains the woman's bowels, her liver, stomach, and so on. But Nature has prevented the egg from becoming lost or going astray by endowing the tubes with the power to ensnare it, almost in the manner of a frog catching a fly. As a matter of fact, the tube's ability to accomplish this feat is developed to such a fine point that if one tube and the opposite ovary have been removed, the remaining tube will still be able to "catch" the egg which has been expelled from the ovary on the other side.

It is the follicle, which held the egg, that is responsible for the production of estrogen, one of the most important female hormones. After the egg has been extruded from it (this phenomenon being known as ovulation), the follicle continues to secrete estrogen and now a second hormone known as progesterone. These two hormones are secreted into the bloodstream, through which they reach the uterus and prepare its lining (the endometrium) for the reception of a fertilized egg. It is this endometrium which is shed every month and comprises the principal constituent of the menstrual flow.

. If the egg is fertilized, the ovary will continue to secrete estrogen and progesterone and menstruation will not occur. If the egg is not fertilized, it will die and, two weeks later, the hormone secretion will cease, menstruation will begin, and the whole cycle will be repeated. Since the human egg remains alive for only twelve hours, women are actually fertile, in the strict sense of the word, for only about six full days a year.

The male of our species displays a different type of inefficiency in his reproductive role. It is his job to provide spermatozoa, a different type of individual cells, which in turn are responsible for finding the egg, penetrating it, and fertilizing it. Instead of being able to discharge these sperm only once a month, he is able to do so every time he has intercourse, and he will provide almost a quarter of a billion of them with every ejaculation. These sperm are much tinier than the eggs, and theirs is indeed a difficult task, for they must find the egg (if there happens to be one available at the time) and fertilize it at the far end of the tube, about eight inches away from the cervix. But sperm are capable of locomotion, and some of them reach their destination in as little as one hour.

Now when a sperm comes into contact with an egg, it actually penetrates the egg's cell membrane and enters the substance of the egg itself. This is the precise moment of fertilization, and it is here that another of nature's minor miracles takes place, for as soon as one of these 250,000,000 sperm enters the solitary egg, the egg becomes impenetrable to all the others. The sex and genetic characteristics of the child that results from this union are determined at this very moment. Here's how:

Every cell in the human body, including the primordial egg and sperm, contains exactly forty-six microscopic bodies known as chromosomes. As the egg matures, its chromosomes become divided into twenty-three identical pairs, one set of which is discarded. As the sperm matures, its chromosomes also become divided into twenty-three pairs, twenty-two of which are identical and one of which is not.

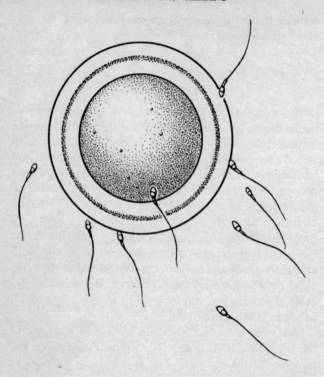

FERTILIZATION OF THE EGG. One of the sperm has penetrated the surface of the egg. Although many thousand times magnified, the relative sizes of the egg and sperm are preserved.

One member of this twenty-third pair is known as an X chromosome and the other as a Y chromosome. The sperm then splits in two, and now the mature sperm, like the mature egg, contains twenty-three chromosomes. So the fertilized egg contains forty-six, twenty-three from the mother and twenty-three from the father. And since it is these chromosomes which carry the genes, the baby that develops from this union will bear genetic similarities (color of hair, size of body, and so forth) to both parents.

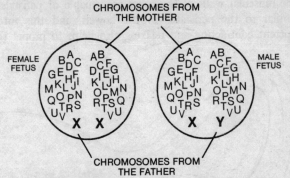

THE DETERMINATION OF SEX. A diagrammatic representation of the forty-six chromosomes in the cells of males and females, showing how the chance combination of an X chromosome from the mother and a Y chromosome from the father results in a boy, whereas an X chromosome from the mother plus an X chromosome from the father result in a girl.

When the sperm splits in two, however, its other half is not discarded. Both halves become mature sperm; one half contains an X chromosome and the other half a Y chromosome. If, as luck will have it, the egg is fertilized by a sperm containing a Y chromosome, the baby will be male; if the sperm contains an X chromosome the baby will be female.

MIGRATION OF THE OVUM

In contrast to the sperm cells, eggs are incapable of locomotion and must depend for their transportation through the tubes and into the uterus upon the action of the tubes themselves. This is accomplished by the tubes through two ingenious devices. First, their interior lining is equipped with millions of infinitesimal hairlike projections (cilia) which are constantly swaying in unison toward the uterus, just like a field of wheat blown by the wind. And second,

the muscular walls of the tubes are capable of peristalsis,
similar to the peristalsis of the bowels, and this intermittent contracting and relaxing also helps to propel the

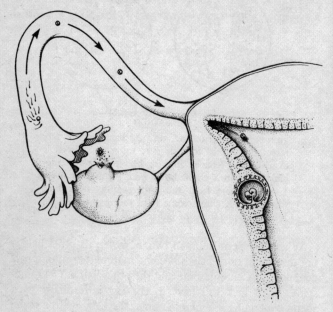

OVULATION TO IMPLANTATION. The egg bursts from the follicle
and is fertilized in the far end of the tube. It begins to divide
during its trip through the tube. The embryo here implanted in
the endometrium is about three weeks old.

egg toward its ultimate destination. If the tubes have ever
been diseased, this mechanism may be interfered with to
such an extent that the egg may become lodged in the
tube itself and an ectopic (from the Greek word for mis-
placed) pregnancy will result. The subject of ectopic pregnancies is discussed in Chapter 5.

If all goes well, as usually happens, the fertilized egg will
reach the uterine cavity in about thirty-six hours, and there
the endometrium will have been properly primed and

thickened by the ovarian hormones so that it will be able to provide the proper succulent bed to nourish this fragile little structure and enable it to grow from an almost weightless, formless object to a seven-pound infant that may be destined some day to share in this same miraculous process by which we perpetuate our race.

THE FETUS, PLACENTA, AND MEMBRANES

For about 270 days this egg is incubated by the human female. This may seem long in comparison with the hamster, whose incubation period is 16 days, or it may seem unfair in comparison to the lady sea horse, whose mate carries the eggs; but, on the brighter side, it is a great deal shorter than the pregnancy of an elephant—624 days.

The initial increase in the size of an egg is accomplished by simple cell division in the same manner by which an amoeba reproduces itself. This process takes place at a fairly rapid pace, so that within a day after the ovum has become embedded in the endometrium it already consists of more than one hundred cells. Twins are discussed in Chapter 5, but it might be well to point out here that it is at approximately this stage in development that identical twins are formed, by the splitting of the ovum into two identical halves. Nonidentical, or fraternal, twins are formed by the simultaneous fertilization of two different eggs.

During these early days in its development the ovum depends for its nourishment upon the absorption of food-stuffs from the endometrium. After a few weeks a distinct organ is formed, the sole purpose of which is absorption of nutriments from and excretion of waste products into the maternal bloodstream. Known as the placenta, or after-birth, this structure is intimately adherent to the uterus on one side and connected to the fetus on the other by the umbilical cord. This cord contains blood vessels which communicate between the fetus and its placenta. These vessels do not communicate with the maternal bloodstream at all, so that the blood of the mother and fetus never mix. Substances are passed back and forth in the placenta between the bloodstreams of mother and fetus by a simple process of diffusion.

Fanning out in all directions from the margin of the placenta and adherent to the inner surface of the uterine wall are the fetal membranes. These membranes comprise a thin, almost transparent sac, much like a balloon, which contains the fetus and the amniotic fluid. This fluid is clear, like water, and by the ninth month there is more than a pint of it. This fluid provides an ideal medium in which the fetus can grow and move about, and it helps to protect the fetus from injury. If you picture the fetus lying in a fluid-filled sac and surrounded by the inch-thick muscular wall of the uterus, which, in turn, is suspended from the bony pelvis by a web of strong but resilient ligaments, you will realize how magnificently it is protected from exterior harm.

The development of the fetus is a complicated process. Suffice it to say that all of its major systems (e.g., the cardiac, respiratory, intestinal, and urinary systems) are more or less formed and functioning by the end of the third month of gestation, by which time the fetus is just beginning to resemble a human being. In many respects these first three months are the most crucial in its formation and development. Since most of the organs are formed at this time, the future normality of the baby is decided right here and now. And if anything does go awry at this early stage, Nature has a ready solution: miscarriage. Most of the fetuses which are destined to be deformed are miscarried. Largely for this reason, nine out of every ten miscarriages occur in the first three months of pregnancy. It is for this reason, too, that a fetus may be damaged if the mother contracts German measles during the first few months (see Chapter 5).

ACTIVITIES OF THE FETUS

Now that its basic anatomical form has been established, the fetus has six more months in which to grow and mature before it can qualify for infancy. During this time it lies curled up in the most compact possible ball, completely surrounded by darkness, warmth, and water. It is hard for us to envision what such a totally aquatic life must be like, even though we all experienced it. We know of course that a fetus moves its arms and legs at irregular, not infrequent intervals. Occasionally it turns completely around, so that one day it may sit right side up and the next day it may stand on its head. It swallows and urinates, but it does not defecate. It wakes, it sleeps, it may have fits of hiccuping, and it may even suck its thumb. After rupture of the membranes (see Chapter 6), fetuses have actually been heard to cry out from the uterus. They must open their eyes occasionally, even though it's too dark to see, and there is reason to believe they can hear a loud noise from the outside world. They don't read their mothers' minds, however, so don't believe the many young wives' tales about a mother's emotions and experiences affecting the unborn baby's personality.

THE SIZE OF THE FETUS

The longer the fetus is incubated in the uterus, the bigger it becomes and the better are its chances for survival. At the end of the fifth month the fetus weighs about one pound; by the end of the sixth month, about two and a quarter pounds; the seventh, four pounds; the eighth, five and a half pounds; and the ninth, seven pounds. You can

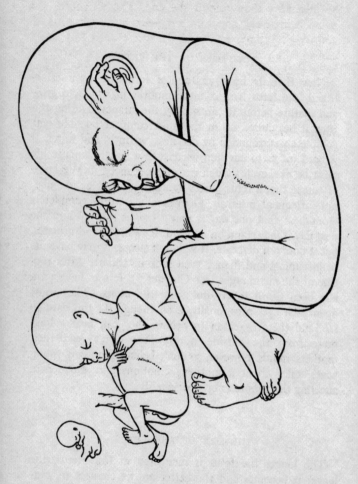

THE GROWING FETUS. Actual size of the fetus in the second, third, and fourth months.

see that the rate of growth is much faster at the beginning of pregnancy than toward the end. The weight of the ovum is increased about 10,000 times in the first month and only 0.3 times in the ninth. But if even this latter, comparatively slow rate were continued after birth, the baby would weigh one hundred and sixty pounds instead of twenty pounds on its first birthday.

Every phase of pregnancy—from ovulation to fertilization to the development of the fetus—is controlled by Nature. There is very little that you can do to improve upon this process and, contrariwise, there is little you can do to damage it. The role of the obstetrician is to promote the naturalness of a normal pregnancy, to prevent aberrations from the norm when possible, and to interfere only in the event of complications.

3

Symptoms and Sensations

During the course of a normal pregnancy most women feel as well as at any other time in their lives; many feel better while pregnant than they ever did before. After all, pregnancy is a perfectly normal state which is remarkable physically mainly in the fact that it involves your carrying around a certain amount of extra weight, mentally in the exhilarating realization that your abdomen contains a new life. There are nevertheless certain minor, common, everyday symptoms and problems which are shared by enough pregnant women to warrant brief discussion.

MORNING SICKNESS

This is one of the most universally recognized symptoms of early pregnancy. About half of womankind would not suspect that they had become pregnant if it were not for the fact that they missed a few periods. The other half, however, complain of morning sickness of varying degrees. This symptom is largely physiological. It is probably caused by the effect of the hormones of pregnancy upon the stomach itself, it usually consists of transient periods of nausea (which may or may not occur in the morning), and it is almost always limited to the first few months of pregnancy. Occasional retching and/or vomiting may occur.

The best way to counteract this annoyance is to eat small amounts frequently, so that your stomach is never empty and yet never overloaded. Dry foods, such as crackers, usually stay down better than liquids, such as soups. Nibble a cracker before you get out of bed in the morning, munch between meals, eat only the foods that appeal to you, and get as much rest as possible. If the nausea persists, tell your doctor about it. He may prescribe a drug or a vitamin. Very rarely does this symptom assume serious proportions; when it does, hospitalization and intravenous feedings are required.

LETHARGY

Another very common complaint of early pregnancy is a feeling of easy fatigability. This symptom, too, is self-limited, usually clearing up after the first few months. Perhaps it is Nature's way of teaching pregnant women to take it a little easy.

FREQUENCY OF URINATION

This is a normal sign during the early months. It is thought to be hormonal in origin and unrelated to pressure on the bladder by the enlarging uterus. Unless associated with a burning sensation it is completely insignificant and requires no treatment. Nocturnal trips to the bathroom may be prevented by reducing the amount of fluid imbibed in the evening.

SWELLING AND TENDERNESS OF THE BREASTS

This is to be expected. It is nothing more than an exaggeration of the swelling and tenderness experienced by many women before the onset of each menstrual period. Good breast support, night and day if necessary, is helpful in reducing the discomfort. It subsides somewhat after the first few months.

Generally speaking, as you might expect, different sensations are characteristic of different stages of pregnancy. It is unusual for any of the above symptoms to persist beyond the third month. The second three-month period (the second trimester) is the most symptom-free. The following are more apt to be noticed as pregnancy progresses:

ABDOMINAL SWELLING

The girth of the abdomen is not usually increased by the enlarging womb until about three and a half to four months have passed. Not infrequently, however, the abdomen seems to be bloated before this, due to a generalized distention of the intestine caused by the pregnancy hormones. This swelling is often more pronounced in parous women (women who have borne children before). Such women may say that they "show more" or "carry lower," since their abdominal walls are weaker and the uterus is therefore more prominent. It is for this reason, too, that parous women often suspect, erroneously, they are going to have twins.

FLATULENCE

The relaxation of the stomach and intestines may be associated with a feeling of bloatedness and more frequent belching, a minor annoyance which may be alleviated by avoiding foods such as cabbage and beans, which tend to produce gas.

HEARTBURN

A burning sensation in the pit of the stomach and lower chest is known as heartburn. It has nothing to do with the heart. It is due to sluggishness of the stomach and regurgitation of the gastric juices. It may be relieved by many of the commercial antacid drugs, by drinking copious amounts of water, or by belladonna prescribed by your doctor. Sodium bicarbonate (and antacid preparations containing sodium) should not be used during pregnancy (see Chapter 4).

QUICKENING

Quickening is an old word denoting fetal movement. If this is your first baby, you will begin to feel it move during the fifth month; if you have already had a baby you may notice it as early as the fourth month. At first it feels faint and fluttery, like butterflies in the stomach, and is difficult to differentiate from one's ordinary intestinal activity, but as the fetus grows, its movements become progressively more strenuous until quite definite kicks and jabs are recognized. These sensations are not painful; after all, the fetus is tiny and is surrounded by water. Fetal activity is usually more noticeable at night, when you are lying quietly in bed. This does not mean that the baby prefers to kick at night, but rather that you are more apt to notice it when you are at rest. It is often said that the fetus becomes less active as labor approaches. To my knowledge this is not true. More regular movement may be caused by the fetus's hiccuping.

Almost without exception, women undergoing their second or third pregnancies feel that "this baby is moving less (or more) than the last one." Even when this is true, it usually augurs nothing with regard to the sex or the well-being of the fetus. As term approaches, however, if fetal activity seems to have slowed down, lie quietly for an hour, count the number of movements, and report your finding to the doctor at the time of your next visit.

SKIN PIGMENTATION

During the second trimester you may begin to notice a darkening of the coloration of your face (the "mask of pregnancy"), your nipples, and the midline of your abdomen. These changes are normal, unpreventable, more marked in brunettes, and they fade away after the baby comes.

LEG CRAMPS

Almost every pregnant woman at one time or another experiences a sudden kink of charley horse in the calf of her leg. These cramps may recur and become rather annoying. They may be due to a deficiency of calcium in the bloodstream or they may be related to the generally sluggish circulation of blood in the pregnant woman's legs. Elevating the foot of the bed may help to prevent the cramps from recurring; heat and massage may help them to disappear. Drinking more milk and keeping the legs propped up whenever possible may prevent them from coming back.

VARICOSE VEINS

The human being became an upright animal before his accomplishments in anatomical evolution included a solution to the problem, created by this newfangled posture, of providing adequate circulation to his lower limbs. As a consequence, the slightest additional strain upon the blood vessels of our legs is apt to result in an unsightly dilatation of the superficial veins, an affliction known as varicose veins. Our mailmen pay for their constant walking and weight lifting by developing varicosities. The same price is often exacted from pregnant women. This condition is rare during a first pregnancy, and once it occurs it gets worse with succeeding pregnancies, but it tends to improve after the birth of the baby. Some women are much more prone to this sort of trouble than others.

The treatment is threefold: preventative, supportive, and curative. All pregnant women should try to prevent varicose veins from developing by propping their legs up on a stool whenever they sit down. It is also helpful to raise the end of the mattress at night in order to promote better circulation. If varicosities develop, the best supportive measure is to wear elastic stockings. These should be worn constantly. If your varicosities are really bad, you may be referred to a surgeon, to see whether they should be injected or removed. This may be done during pregnancy or postponed until after delivery.

HEMORRHOIDS

Hemorrhoids or piles are yet another manifestation of the poor circulation of blood in the lower half of the body during pregnancy. Hemorrhoids are nothing more or less than varicosities of the rectum. Especially common during the last months of pregnancy, they consist of a rosette of purplish protuberances around the anus or in the lower portion of the rectum, which may cause bleeding or pain during defecation. The most important principle in prevention and treatment is the maintenance of normal bowel function. Constipation, diarrhea, and straining at stool will aggravate the situation. Pain relief may be obtained through sitz baths, manual replacement of the hemorrhoids into the rectum, the application of pads containing witch hazel, or the use of anesthetic suppositories and ointments prescribed by your doctor. Hemorrhoids become most troublesome during the first week after delivery; they then regress spontaneously.

CONSTIPATION

A common concomitant of pregnancy, constipation is ascribed to the sluggishness of the intestinal tract. Increasing the amount of roughage (fruits, vegetables, cereals) in the diet is the simplest means of alleviating this condition. If this proves insufficient, however, there is no harm in the occasional use of any of the common cathartics except castor oil (which may cause uterine contractions). More stubborn cases are helped by various new stool-softening medications which your doctor can prescribe. If your bowel movements become black during pregnancy it is probably due to the iron you are taking.

BACKACHE

The strain of bearing the unaccustomed weight of pregnancy, combined with the relaxation of the pelvic joints during pregnancy, not infrequently results in a mild but annoying ache in the lower back. Relief can usually be achieved through rest, Tylenol, and the local application of heat in the form of a hot-water bottle or heating pad. More persistent cases may respond to wearing a maternity girdle or placing a bedboard (a piece of plywood or a door) under the mattress.

GROIN PAINS

Probably the most universal site of discomfort in pregnancy is the groin. During any stage of pregnancy you may feel a mild achy sensation in one or both sides of the lower abdomen. These pains characteristically come and go.

They are probably due to the stretching of the ligaments which support the uterus, one of which (the round ligament) runs along each groin. They may be helped by prepared-childbirth exercises or by wearing a maternity girdle.

STRIAE

The striae, or red markings, on the skin of the abdomen and breasts, especially during a first pregnancy, are another sign of the stretching process. There is little that one can do about them, although some women claim some benefit from anointing their skin with baby oils or cocoa butter. These marks become smaller after delivery and eventually assume an almost silvery color, but they do not completely disappear.

NOSEBLEEDS

There is an increase in the blood supply to all of the mucous membranes during pregnancy. The lining of the nostrils is no exception. Its blood vessels often break and cause nosebleeds, especially during the winter months when we live in the hot, dry atmosphere of central heating. If your nose bleeds, put your head back, apply pressure to your upper lip, put a cold compress against the back of your neck, and avoid irritating your nose in the future. A little Boroleum jelly or white Vaseline will help keep the mucous membranes from drying out.

ANGIOMAS

Occasionally pregnant women notice what are known medically as "spider angiomas" on their skin, most often on the shoulders, arms, and face. These are tiny red marks which, when examined closely, are seen to consist of minute blood vessels arranged radially in somewhat the shape of a spider. Caused by the pregnancy hormones, they largely disappear after delivery.

FAINTNESS AND DIZZINESS

A large proportion of a pregnant woman's blood volume becomes pooled in her abdomen in order to supply the needs of the fetus. During pregnancy there is also a relative anemia, due to the demands of the fetus for maternal iron. For these reasons the circulation of oxygen-rich blood to the brain of the gravid woman is at times slightly deficient and episodes of dizziness and faintness may result. Often these episodes are precipitated by a sudden change in position or they may occur in a crowded bus or department store. They are usually brief and self-limited and may be curtailed by sitting with the head between the knees or by lying down. Loss of consciousness is rare. If you are subject to such attacks, you might want to carry some smelling salts in your purse.

INSOMNIA

Pregnant women often have difficulty getting to sleep. This is understandable, I think, on two counts. In the first place, pregnancy provokes a great many new thoughts and challenges in a woman's mind; and secondly, during the latter months the desire to sleep may be thwarted by inability to assume a comfortable position and by the baby's kicking. This sleeplessness rarely warrants medical attention unless it is severe, in which case your doctor may prescribe a mild sedative. (You cannot, incidentally, injure the fetus by lying on your abdomen.)

MOODINESS

Any cause of emotional upheaval, such as pregnancy, is bound to produce alterations in personality. The extent and duration of these alterations depend largely upon the psychological makeup of the individual and the success she has had in adjusting to society. Accordingly obstetricians frequently hear that a patient has become irritable or depressed. This information is sometimes volunteered by the patient; more often it emanates from the husband.* Usually these problems are mild and they respond rapidly to discussion with the husband or doctor. Occasionally they are serious enough to warrant psychiatric attention.

SHORTNESS OF BREATH

Toward the end of pregnancy slight shortness of breath may be experienced, especially on exertion. The obvious explanation of this is that the enlarging uterus presses up against the diaphragm and renders it less mobile. The solution is equally obvious: less exertion, especially lifting and stair climbing. If it occurs at night, prop your shoulders up on a couple of pillows.

VAGINAL DISCHARGE

This common annoyance is normal in the late months of pregnancy, when a clear odorless liquid is secreted by the congested mucous membrane of the vagina. If the dis-

---

* Throughout this book I have referred to the male as a "husband," though I recognize and respect the fact that this may be technically inaccurate in some cases. "Partner," however, seems stilted and "father" doesn't always sound right. It is not always easy to find the apt word.

charge is copious, malodorous, or associated with itching it probably indicates the presence of vaginal inflammation and should be reported to your doctor. Although difficult to eradicate during pregnancy, it can be kept under control by proper medication and it characteristically disappears after delivery.

SWOLLEN ANKLES

The tissues of the body retain increasing amounts of fluid toward the end of pregnancy. Together with the impeded circulation of blood in the legs, this tendency is frequently responsible for swelling of the ankles. Whereas this may be a trivial symptom by itself, especially in the hot summer months, it may also portend the development of toxemia (see Chapter 5) and hence should be reported to your doctor. This is especially true if the swelling proceeds to involve other areas of the body, such as the hands and face. Restriction of dietary salt is the most effective means of preventing and combating this condition. In unresponsive cases the doctor may prescribe the temporary use of a diuretic, which will increase the rate of excretion of fluids in the urine.

HUSBANDS' SYMPTOMS

Some husbands experience morning sickness and other empathic symptoms when their wives are pregnant. If your husband seems too wretched, buy him a teddy bear.

4

Rules and Regulations

In general there is no reason why a pregnant woman should significantly modify her accustomed way of life. Whatever restrictions may be imposed by the pregnant state are largely based on common sense and an overall awareness that there is a being-in-the-making whose welfare has to be taken into consideration. Let's look at some guidelines which may help you.

DIET

When your grandmother was pregnant she was told to eat for two. On this advice she gained fifty pounds. And she knew nothing about vitamins. Your mother was told to gain no more than twenty pounds. She knew a lot about vitamins, but neither she nor her obstetrician knew much about fetal nutrition. Now we know that your grandmother's fetus was probably overfed (not to mention your grandmother) and your mother's fetus (you) ran the risk of malnutrition.

Total Weight Gain. In modern obstetrics the emphasis is placed more on fetal welfare than on maternal weight, for if the fetus is not well fed it may be born malnourished or even defective. On the other hand, the mother's weight gain cannot be ignored, for it is an index of maternal and fetal health: too little and the fetus may suffer, too much and you may develop complications such as toxemia, which may in turn also affect the baby adversely. There can be no strict rule governing weight limits, applicable to every woman. Your obstetrician will give you guidance based on your particular needs. Perhaps the closest one can come to a weight-gain rule is that if you begin your pregnancy at a weight ideal for your body frame you should be about twenty-four pounds heavier when you deliver.

These twenty-four pounds are neatly accounted for in the following table (obviously, they and other figures on weight and calories are approximate):

Baby	7½ pounds
Placenta	1½ pounds
Amniotic Fluid	2 pounds
Uterus (increase in size)	2½ pounds
Breasts (increase in size)	2 pounds
Blood (increase in volume)	3½ pounds
Fat and Fluid	5 pounds
Total	24 pounds

The first five pounds of fat and fluid will be lost, together with the other tabulated poundage, at or soon after delivery. Any additional fat will be all yours.

Rate of Weight Gain. So how are you going to arrive at the nine-month weight limit recommended by your doctor, at the same time fortify yourself and your fetus with all the right dietary ingredients—and still enjoy your food? Actually, if your weight is nearly right for your height you can probably continue to eat the same *quantity* of food that you habitually consume. Of greater concern will be its *quality*, to insure proper fetal development. Ideally, then, you will gain about three pounds in the first three months and about three quarters of a pound a week thereafter.

Acceptable Monthly Weight Gain

A. 100, 103, 106, 110, 114, 118, 123, 128, 134, 140
B. 120, 121, 122, 124, 126, 129, 132, 136, 140, 144
C. 195, 196, 197, 198, 200, 202, 204, 206, 208, 212

WEIGHT GAIN. Acceptable monthly increments for three women, 5 feet 6 inches tall, who tip the scales before pregnancy at 100, 120, and 195 pounds respectively.

If you are overweight your caloric consumption may have to be curtailed. This can be done, with constant attention to the quality of food ingested, without endangering the pregnancy. You will be allowed to gain, but the limit may be set as low as fifteen pounds.

Dietary Guides. I have a confession to make: I can't stand most of the advice I read about dieting. Many Helpful Hannahs tell you how to plan a menu: "For breakfast, one glass of vitamin-enriched low-fat milk, two wafers of rye crisp, two thirds pat of butter . . ." Now who can plan meals like that? Other manuals list categories of food you must eat every day: "At least one of the following nutritious vegetables: kohlrabi, rutabaga, dandelion greens . . ." Now who among you eats kohlrabi? Others admonish: "At least six glasses of water daily." Who can drink all that water (in addition to those "eight glasses of low-fat, vitamin-enriched milk")? Others tell you how many grams or "servings" you must eat. But who, other than pharmacists, knows from grams, and who can define a serving?

Surely more general guidelines will suffice, at least for the vast majority. And if you have an unusual dietary problem your doctor will deal with it or send you to a nutritionist. So let me give you some basic information and permit you to plan your own menus and measure your own slices.

Calories. The basic truth here is that, because of the metabolic changes in her body and the demands of her growing fetus, a pregnant woman needs more calories than she did before she conceived—about 15 percent more. Although I don't expect you to sit down and compute your caloric intake, if you are about five-foot-four and 120 pounds, it should be in the neighborhood of 2,100 before pregnancy and 2,400 while pregnant.

Protein. As you know, there are three categories of food: protein, carbohydrate, and fat. The principal building block in constructing fetal and other new tissue is protein.

So this is the category to be stressed—indeed, almost doubled—in pregnancy. Most of it must come from animal sources: milk (ideally a quart a day), cheese, meat, fish, and eggs. If you can't drink a quart of milk, you should cook with it or consume it in the form of other diary products. Vegetable sources of protein (beans, whole grains, peanut butter) are useful supplements, but not sufficient unto themselves.

Carbohydrate. Fruits and vegetables are essential. Starches and sweets are not. It is as simple as that. So stress the citruses, the salads, and the legumes, which are rich sources of energy and vitamins; skip the Coke and cake; and be sure your bread is whole grain or vitamin-enriched.

Fat. Each morsel of fat provides more than twice the calories in a comparable-sized morsel of carbohydrate or protein. It is an unavoidable component in any protein-rich diet, so don't seek it from other sources—i.e., go easy on the butter, oleo, salad dressing, and cooking oils.

Iron. Iron is needed in great quantities in pregnancy, in order to build and maintain the oxygen-carrying red blood cells in the maternal and fetal circulatory systems. It is found in most meats (and especially in liver), turkey, spinach, egg yolks, clams and oysters, rolled oats, and whole wheat bread. Although more easily absorbed from food than from pills, it is rarely present in adequate amounts even in a well-planned pregnancy diet, so you must take your prenatal capsules regularly in addition to eating your liver and spinach.

Calcium. Calcium is necessary for the formation of fetal bone and teeth. Its primary source is, of course, milk. In pill form it is less well absorbed from the intestinal tract. Hence another reason to drink that quart of cow's milk—or consume an equivalent amount of other dairy products.

Fluoride. The ingestion of fluoride during infancy and childhood will prevent dental caries. It is not yet known whether the ingestion of fluoride during pregnancy will

further protect the progeny's teeth. Until this issue is settled, I would err on the side of taking prenatal capsules
with fluoride, especially in areas where the water is not
fluoridated. Ask your doctor about it.

Vitamins. This country is vitamin crazy. I would bet
that 99 percent of all the vitamin pills consumed by Amer-
icans every year are completely unnecessary. True, we all
need vitamins; but, pregnant or not, we rarely need more
of them than those provided by three well-balanced meals
a day. There are occasional exceptions, where the need
is excessive (in cases of anemia, for example, and in twin
pregnancies) and a small surplus won't hurt you. By and
large, though, vitamins are the least important component
in those prenatal pills.

Salt. The more salt you eat, the more water your body
will retain, and pregnant women are prone to retaining
water, so salt should be used in moderation. There is
plenty of it hidden in processed meats and cheeses, canned
vegetables, condiments, and cereals. Not to mention salted
nuts and crackers, bacon and ham. So give the saltcellar a
rest while you are pregnant. And since it is the sodium in
salt (sodium chloride) that we are talking about, you
should also avoid sodium bicarbonate (often used as an
antacid) and monosodium glutamate (often prevalent in
Chinese food).

Food Preparation. The caloric content of food is increased by frying. It is better to boil, broil, or roast. And
the vitamins and minerals in fruits and vegetables are
slowly lost in the process of cooking, soaking, or even exposure to the air. It is therefore preferable to eat fruits and
vegetables fresh and raw or, if you cook them, it is better
to steam them. While cooking with milk, the evaporated
or powdered variety is just as nourishing as the real thing.
For drinking purposes remember that skim milk contains
all of the protein, calcium, and iron found in whole milk,
with only about half the calories. Sugar and salt substi-
tutes should be used only on your doctor's recommendation.

Special Problems

Teenagers. The pregnant teenager presents a dietary problem for two reasons: (1) Like the fetus, she is still growing. Hence her baseline needs for calories, protein, vitamins, and minerals are higher than her older sister's. And (2) today's teenagers tend to eat junk foods and to pursue fad diets which are not permissible in pregnancy. Your obstetrician should give you special dietary counseling if you are under eighteen.

Vegetarians. Of course you have the right to your own dietary pursuits when only your body is concerned. Not so, however, when a fetus is also being nourished by what you eat. Meat and milk are musts in any pregnancy diet. Vegetarian diets are deficient in protein, vitamin B_{12}, iron, and calcium.

Snackers. Raiding the icebox at night, sneaking a cookie between meals, and sipping calorie-laden soft drinks to quell a hunger pang are not good practices for pregnant women. If you have this kind of habit and can't kick it, you must deduct the calories you consume in this way from those you consume at mealtimes. Better yet, substitute raw vegetables, such as carrots and celery, for those superfluous sweets.

Nursing Mothers. The nursing mother's requirements for calories, vitamins, and fluids are somewhat greater than they were when she was pregnant. The need for iron and calcium is unchanged. She should increase from one quart to one and a fourth quarts her consumption of milk (or an equivalent amount of other dairy products). And she should be sure to protect her baby's teeth with fluoride—in the water she drinks and/or in her vitamin pills.

A Final Word. Despite the simplicity of these general guidelines, many pregnant women tend to gain too much weight. Regular daily exercise can, of course, help to counteract this tendency. If you are exercising, eating sensibly, and still gaining too much, review your diet with your obstetrician. Ultimately, though, the responsibility for what you eat is yours alone. How you discharge this responsibility will determine the nutritional status of your baby.

CIGARETTES, ALCOHOL, AND DRUGS

Alcoholism is known to cause abnormalities of the fetus. Even the regular ingestion of cocktails is to be avoided, for it can reduce your baby's birth weight. An occasional drink is probably harmless.

Women who smoke during pregnancy tend to have smaller babies and, in general, the heavier the smoking the smaller the baby is apt to be. There is also evidence that the fetal death rate is higher among women who smoke. If you are a smoker, it is imperative that you cut your consumption to no more than half a pack a day. Better yet, for your sake and your baby's, cut it out.

The effect on pregnancy of smoking marijuana (or even inhaling the smoke from someone else's joint) is not yet known. There is, however, reason to suspect that it might cause genetic damage to future generations—i.e., to your grandchildren. For these nine months, then, you had better get your highs from more old-fashioned sources.

Even the use of bona fide FDA-approved medications must be carefully monitored during pregnancy, for most drugs which affect the mother will affect the fetus too. Aspirin can alter the blood-clotting mechanism, phenobarbital can produce fetal abnormalities, tetracycline (a commonly used antibiotic) can cause permanent discoloration of the offspring's teeth, and sulfa drugs taken late in pregnancy can damage the baby's brain. Check with your doctor before taking pills of any kind. .

DOUCHING, INTERCOURSE, AND TUB BATHS

It is almost impossible to inflict damage upon a fetus lying in a womb. It is so well protected by fluid and membranes and the womb itself, as well as the abdominal wall and the bony pelvis, that it is virtually immune to injury.

This being true, it follows that the simple acts of douching and sexual intercourse can hardly be expected to cause trouble. It is said that there is wisdom in refraining from intercourse at the time of the first three expected periods, that is, at the time when these periods would have occurred in the absence of pregnancy, but even this belief is without foundation. It is probably advisable to abstain during the last few weeks of pregnancy, not so much because of the fear of injury as because of the possibility of introducing bacteria into the birth canal at a time when labor may be imminent. Sometimes, of course, these general rules must be modified to suit an individual case.

There is no sense in douching during pregnancy (or at any other time, for that matter) unless there is a specific reason. If you notice an unusual amount of discharge or a feeling of irritation in the region of the vagina, you should consult your obstetrician. He may recommend a douche, and there is no danger in douching during pregnancy if you know how. Generally speaking, the most effective and economical solution with which to douche consists of two tablespoons of white vinegar in a quart of warm water. You should lie down on your back in the bathtub with the douche bag suspended no more than two feet above the bottom of the tub. The nozzle should be introduced no more than two or three inches into the vagina. A bulb syringe should never be used.

The only harm that might result from taking a shower or a tub bath at any time during pregnancy is that the pregnant woman, in her top-heavy state, might slip and fall on the tile. Ideally there should be a grab bar on the wall and a rubber mat on the bottom of the tub. Believe it or not, water does not enter the vagina during a tub bath.

WORK

Since riveting and ditchdigging are rarely performed by American women, there is almost no field of endeavor which cannot be pursued during pregnancy in this country. Surely no harm will come to you from washing or drying the dishes or from giving or taking dictation. The principal detriment to be derived from work is the fatigue involved, and this usually stems from commuting back and forth or from prolonged sitting in one position. Aside from this fatigue there is no reason why pregnant women shouldn't work until at least the seventh month. During the last four to six weeks of pregnancy many working women are given a vacation with pay.

REST

To say that a pregnant woman needs eight hours' sleep is platitudinous. Everyone needs eight hours' sleep. The requirements for rest during pregnancy are basically no different from those in the nonpregnant state. During the last six or eight weeks, however, the pregnant woman may tire more easily, especially if she has children to care for. She will then profit from an afternoon nap.

EXERCISE

There are three types of physical exercise to be considered during pregnancy: the everyday activities such as walking, the more strenuous exertion of sports, and the formal calisthenics such as those recommended in natural-childbirth programs. It would, of course, be wise to avoid deep-sea diving, mountain climbing, and bullfighting, but there is no harm inherent in swimming or tennis or touching your toes. (Nor will your stooping or stretching cause the fetus to be strangled by its umbilical cord.) Violent exercise, in other words, is to be avoided. Moderate exercise is beneficial: it will help you to retain your figure and it will prepare you for the rigors of labor.

Sports. If you are proficient at tennis or swimming or even horseback riding, go to it. Your common sense will dictate that you avoid rough terrain in riding, for falls of any kind are to be avoided. And you will hardly want to take up a new and vigorous sport such as skiing at this time. There is debate about the advisability of jogging during pregnancy; ask your doctor what he thinks.

Calisthenics. Calisthenics seem to appeal to some people more than others. If you are fond of chinning yourself or touching your toes, this kind of exercise, performed regularly, can help to keep you fit. Ask your doctor for a list of calisthenics particularly suited to pregnant women. After delivery they are most helpful in restoring muscle tone.

Formalized exercises constitute an integral part of natural-childbirth programs. Women are told how to relax during contractions in the first stage of labor, how to bear down with contractions in the second stage. These are not "exercises" in the normal sense; they are not meant to strengthen muscles. Rather they are intended (1) to inform the woman so that she will know how to participate in the labor process, (2) to condition her so that it will be easier for her to perform these simple functions under stress, and (3) to distract her so that she will concentrate upon what she is doing rather than upon what is happening to her. In a sense, then, the ritualistic performance of these exercises amounts to a form of self-hypnosis. This is not meant to belittle them, for they are most helpful, whether they are hypnotic or not.

One of the tenets of the British and American schools of natural childbirth is that the mother should learn how to breathe with her diaphragm rather than her chest during first-stage contractions. Proof of the fact that psychology plays a more important role than physiology in the rationale of these exercises lies in the fact that the French and Russian schools insist that chest rather than abdominal breathing is beneficial, yet all four schools are equally successful in accomplishing the same aim.

TRAVEL

In general, travel is permissible during pregnancy, but several factors must be considered first, such as the length of the trip, the mode of transportation, and the stage of pregnancy. It is doubtful that a long car ride, for example, will induce a miscarriage or incite the onset of labor; but what are you to do if you start to bleed or if your water does break or if you do go into labor 500 or 1,000 miles from home? These and other accidents can happen unexpectedly at any time or place, and it is sometimes quite a mess when they happen where medical care is unavailable or where the doctor that you do find is strange to you and vice versa.

For this reason, if no other, it is wise when you are pregnant (1) not to take unnecessary trips, (2) not to go too far or for too long a time, (3) to find a new doctor if you plan to stay put for a while away from home, (4) to arrange your trips during the middle months of pregnancy when you are least likely to abort or to deliver, and (5) to show preference for plane rather than train, and train rather than car. It is also advisable, if you must go by car, to travel a maximum of about 200 miles per day and to stop frequently in order to get kinks out of your back and legs. Don't go farther than 100 miles during the last month. And consult the airline before making a reservation late in pregnancy; some of them have regulations against taking too-pregnant passengers.

MOVING AND PAINTING

In planning for an addition to the family, many expectant parents find it necessary to move into larger quarters or at least to redecorate the ones they have. It stands to reason, therefore, that if moving or redecorating is harmful to pregnant women a great many pregnant women are being harmed, and this, in turn, seems unlikely. It is obvious that a pregnant woman should not take a very active part in the actual moving process. She is already carrying her share of the weight. So let the men do the work.

Fresh paint was unhealthy for the pregnant and the nonpregnant alike in the days when most paint contained lead. In these days of rubber-based paint and water-based paint this risk no longer exists.

CLOTHES

There seems little point in reminding you that pregnant women should dress comfortably and attractively. But there are a few minor matters worth mentioning in this connection.

Circular garters interfere with circulation of the blood in the legs. Don't wear them. Wear panty hose or a garter belt. Or go bare-legged.

As noted in Chapter 3, many pregnant women develop varicose veins. The best treatment for this condition, aside from elevation of the legs, is elastic stockings. Elastic stockings are not pretty, but they are a healthful temporary measure; varicose veins are not pretty, but they are permanent and unhealthy. If you wear elastic stockings, wear them all the time in spite of your vanity. Generally speaking, the thicker and uglier they are the more effective they are.

Good support of the breasts during pregnancy is important during the first few and the last few months, when the breasts swell the most. So invest early in some good strong maternity brassieres and wear them at these times—night and day if your breasts are at all uncomfortable. Take them to the hospital, too, for you will need them while you are learning to nurse.

Flat-heeled shoes put less strain on the back in pregnancy. They also make for a little safer walking. They are, therefore, somewhat preferable to high-heeled shoes; but, on the other hand, many strong-backed, well-balanced women wear high heels for nine months and seem to get away with it.

Wear loose-fitting clothes. Don't try to hide your pregnancy. Pregnant women are beautiful.

TEETH

The fetus needs calcium to form bone. That's why you should drink milk and/or take calcium pills. But even without these precautions, the fetus is not going to rob your teeth of their calcium; it will harmlessly pilfer the stuff from your bones. So don't listen to your grandmother's admonition about "a tooth for every child." It is nonetheless sensible to see your dentist early in pregnancy, for it is especially important to be in good health from head to toe when two lives depend on it. If your dentist wants to fill or pull your teeth or give you Novocain, let him; if he wants to give you gas, consult your obstetrician first.

BREAST AND SKIN CARE

The stretch marks or striae which form on breasts and abdomen are unpreventable. They are one of the badges of motherhood. If the stretching of the skin causes any discomfort, however, feel free to anoint yourself with lanolin or cocoa butter or baby oil; these might help. If your skin itches, tell your doctor.

Ordinarily no preparation is necessary to ready the breasts for nursing. If your nipples are inverted (turned in or unduly flat), it is probably worthwhile to draw them out manually every day during the last few months. Rubbing lanolin into the nipple area will help to make this easier to do. There is also a plastic doughnut-shaped device which may be worn under the bra to correct this condition.

VACCINATIONS

Presumably you have been vaccinated against poliomyelitis (infantile paralysis) by now. If not, this would be a good time to have this done.

You are also probably immune to rubella (German measles), either because you had the disease as a child or because you were vaccinated against it as you were growing up. If you are not immune, this cannot be rectified while you are pregnant, for the vaccine, given during pregnancy or the three months before conception, may cause fetal deformities.

Influenza vaccine is generally not given to pregnant women, because it is neither terribly effective nor totally harmless.

If other vaccinations are needed during pregnancy—e.g., for trips abroad—consult your obstetrician about their safety.

SEX OF THE BABY

There is no practical way to predict the sex of the baby. Curiosity on this score has led people throughout history to invent means to solve this puzzle. The size of the mother's breasts, the color of her face, and scores of other ridiculous criteria have been used. It is widely believed today that the obstetrician can tell by looking at an X-ray of the fetus or listening to its heartbeat, but these ideas are equally erroneous. There is one accurate method, which involves puncturing the membranes and examining fetal cells in the amniotic fluid (amniocentesis); but this procedure is recommended only for the evaluation of fetal well-being

—especially for the detection of hereditary diseases (see Chapter 1). Ironically, when the sex of the fetus is revealed to the doctor, during the fifth month, as an incidental result of this test, and the doctor offers to share this information with his patient, fully 50 percent of women do not want to know the sex of their baby-to-be.

This may be a good place to dispel the notion that it is the woman who is responsible for the sex of her offspring. In olden times, you will remember from high school history, kings used to banish or behead their wives for not producing a male heir to the throne. As you can see from the description of the sex chromosomes in Chapter 2, however, the rationale for this extreme in macho behavior was ill-founded, for it is the male sperm, even of kings, that is solely responsible for the sex of our progeny.

THE FATHER AND THE GRANDMOTHER

The Father. It is hoped that prospective fathers as well as mothers will read this book. Those of you who do so will already have proved your interest in the pregnancy, so it would be superfluous for me to remind you that this pregnancy is half yours. As for a more precise definition of your role, this should be pretty much instinctive. The simple truth must be equally obvious to both of us, namely, that no matter how active you would like to be in sharing this experience with your wife your role became indisputably passive the moment the egg was fertilized, or shortly before. Your job now is to manifest just the right combination of husbandly attentiveness, masculine reserve, paternal devotion, and scientific curiosity.

A few tips: remind her to take her vitamins, don't scold her for forgetting; encourage her to watch her diet, don't chide her for overeating; buy her maternity clothes, don't criticize her appearance. You can't carry the fetus, but you can press your ear to it and hear its heartbeat. You can't experience the labor, or delivery, but you can at least demonstrate the right amount of interest, sympathy, or pride in what's going on. You can buy her flowers after it's over, you can help ready the house for the arrival of your wife and baby, and you can learn to change and bathe the baby. Perhaps "in the old country" the husband did none of these things. But this is twentieth-century America, where the husband is expected to help out.

The Grandmother. As for prospective grandmothers, it is difficult to convince some of them that their role has become a passive one and it is impossible to convince others that they should play any role at all. Rare is the pregnant woman's mother who knows when to come in and when to stay out of the picture. But now is the time for you to try to define your mother's role in your life if you haven't already and if you ever hope to. Often this step requires courage on the part of the prospective mother and her parent. Suffice it to say that if you're going to have a baby you're grown up. Don't bring your mother to the doctor's office every time, don't live with her if you can help it, and don't listen to her advice in preference to your obstetrician's. Maybe you've been married only a few months and you've lived all of your life under your mother's wing. Well, now your primary duty is to your husband and your unborn baby, not to your mother, and this is an opportune time to make this clear to all concerned.

Does this attitude seem cruel to you? Most women won't need this advice at all; it is for those of you who think it is cruel that this advice is intended. You are not a baby anymore; you are going to have a baby. Some day your child will grow up and leave you too. This is the framework of our civilization: the marriage unit.

Oh, I almost forgot your mother-in-law. Perhaps you would like to forget her too. Don't. She is also a part of this production. So let her say her lines without being constantly upstaged by you and your mom. If you assign her the right role you might even like her performance.

If your husband is a student and doesn't have a dime, he should work nights and you should work too. You'll be happier in the long run if you can (and you can) assume financial as well as emotional independence of your parents. If they are well-to-do and insist on buying you a washing machine, you might do well to accept with thanks, but don't let them subsidize your whole pregnancy.

And finally we come to the paradox whereby most new mothers need some immediate help when they first bring the baby home. Call on Grandmother now, by all means. This is what she is for. She can be a source of great comfort and aid during the first week or two of motherhood. She can help with the cooking and the dusting, she can show you how to change a diaper, and she can tell you how you cried all night for the first three months. But it's your baby. Remember that. Don't raise your child exactly as your mother raised you.

PACKING A BAG

Some time during the last month of pregnancy every woman seems mysteriously compelled to pack a bag. This is an instinctive compulsion which baffles most men, including me, but its very universality seems to justify it.

Regardless of any preconceived ideas you might have about labor-room activities, I can assure you that you will need none of your own belongings while you are in labor. As a matter of fact, upon your very first encounter with a labor-room nurse she will ask you to relinquish all of your clothes, jewelry, and even your false teeth. Leave your valuables at home. You will be given a hospital gown, which is much more practical than your own nightie. Even if you are to have your baby in a birthing room, where you can wear your prettiest negligee, you would be wise to exchange your lovely silk gown for the regulation cotton sack.

After you return to your own room you may prefer to have your own maternity brassieres, nightgowns, bathrobe, slippers, cosmetics, toilet articles, and reading material. If not, however, the hospital can probably supply you with most of these things and it will surely provide clothes for the baby and a limitless supply of soap, sheets, and sanitary napkins. In most hospitals, radios and television sets can be rented, books borrowed, and newspapers subscribed to. Hospitals are a lot like hotels in many ways; they are usually equipped to cater to the simplest and the most exacting tastes. You will, of course, need clothes for yourself and the baby when you leave the hospital, but your husband can bring them to you.

So pack your bag, pack it a month early, and put into it whatever you like. If in the last minute rush you forget to take it with you, you will probably get along just as well without it, but in the meanwhile it will serve to symbolize the inevitable end of the pregnancy process.

5

*Complications
of Pregnancy*

Most young women of childbearing age enjoy good general health. They may develop minor annoyances such as hemorrhoids or heartburn during pregnancy, but serious complications are rare. There are, however, a few diseases, such as toxemia, which are peculiar to pregnancy, and, of course, any chronic illness, such as diabetes, may coincide with pregnancy. Although the main purpose of this book is to emphasize the normality of the pregnant state, several secondary ends may be served by presenting brief descriptions of the more common complications. Through even a cursory understanding of them, you should be better equipped to appreciate the normal, to recognize the abnormal, to act in an emergency, and to assess the significance of any problem you might encounter.

Generally speaking, women who become pregnant for the first time after the age of thirty-five are slightly more prone to develop complications. Many women have completely normal, uneventful first pregnancies at thirty-six or thirty-nine or even forty-two, but in this age range they do have to be watched a little more carefully.

This might be a good place to insert a statement which

needs more emphasis than you might imagine, namely, that no two pregnancies are alike. If you were terribly nauseated with your first pregnancy it does not follow that you will be nauseated with this one. That you gained thirty pounds without developing toxemia the first time does not assure you of such good fortune again. Nor will this fetus necessarily kick so much as the last one. Nor is your labor going to be the same. There are, of course, general trends, such as the fact that some women tend to deliver prematurely, and varicose veins are apt to become worse with each pregnancy, and kidney infections are prone to recur. But by and large the course of each pregnancy will be quite different from the others of the same individual.

MISCARRIAGES

The terms miscarriage and spontaneous abortion are synonymous in medical parlance. These words are used to describe the termination of a pregnancy before the baby is big enough to survive. Miscarriages are very common. At least one out of every ten pregnancies terminates in this manner.

Causes. Most miscarriages result from the union of sperm with an imperfect egg or vice versa. No matter how healthy the man and woman, a certain number of his sperm and her eggs are bound to be faulty and, as pointed out in Chapter 2, the pregnancies which result from such a union are usually aborted. There is nothing whatever that can be done to prevent this. Occasionally abortions are due to a maternal disease, such as hypothyroidism or diabetes, or a congenital deformity of the pelvic organs, the treatment of which may prevent future abortions. But usually miscarriages are unpreventable and of no particular significance in the overall reproductive potential of a healthy young woman.

It is virtually impossible for any sort of body injury to cause a miscarriage. Likewise it stands to reason that if some such normal function as intercourse or douching or riding in a car seems to have precipitated a miscarriage, then such a pregnancy was certainly doomed from the start and the miscarriage would have occurred in this case sooner or later anyway. In short, if a miscarriage occurs, there is nothing to be gained by searching for an outside cause to feel guilty about. These things are beyond your control.

Despite the fact that you can't prevent a miscarriage, you might be able to learn something from the event: if you miscarry, save the tissue expelled from your vagina and ask your doctor to send it to one of the special labs which have recently been set up to perform genetic studies on this material. If a congenital abnormality is detected, you will be in need of genetic counseling about future pregnancies.

Time of Occurrence. Nine out of ten miscarriages occur during the first three months of pregnancy, so once you have reached this point you can pretty much dismiss this fear. And contrariwise, since so many pregnancies do end in early abortion, it is wise not to feel overly confident until you have passed the third month. It is probably for this reason that many women don't spread the happy news among their friends until they are a little further along.

Symptoms. The cardinal signs of miscarriage are pain and bleeding. The pain comes in the form of lower abdominal cramps, similar to menstrual cramps or early labor pains. The bleeding is usually bright red, sometimes brown; it may be scant or copious. If either of these symptoms occurs, go to bed and call your doctor, in that order. If you pass anything which looks like tissue, save it and show it to your doctor. If the tissue includes the fetus or part of the placenta the abortion process has become irreversible.

Sometimes these symptoms appear briefly and then disappear on their own. At least one in five women bleed during the early months of pregnancy, but only half of these go on to abort. The other half stop bleeding and carry to term normally. By and large, however, once bleeding occurs, abortion will or will not follow, regardless of what either you or your doctor does. Bed rest, sedation, and hormones are often prescribed after the bleeding has started, but there is no convincing evidence that any of these remedies has ever prevented an abortion. So by all means follow your doctor's instructions, but pray, too, that you are one of the lucky ones whose bleeding will spontaneously stop.

Treatment. The process of abortion is sometimes incomplete. Fragments of placental tissue may remain in the uterus and bleeding will continue until they are removed. For this reason it is necessary in some cases to perform a curettage (a scraping), thereby evacuating the uterine cavity completely. This is a minor operation which is performed in the hospital. In other cases the entire pregnancy may be aborted in toto and the administration of a drug such as Ergotrate, which will cause the uterus to contract, will suffice to prevent unnecessary blood loss.

Late abortions (i.e., those occurring between the twelfth and twentieth weeks) are more hazardous and will therefore usually require hospitalization.

Recovery. Recovery from a miscarriage should be prompt and permanent if the blood loss was not excessive. And when it comes to interpreting the phrase "excessive blood loss," bear in mind the fact that it is not harmful for a healthy person to donate a pint of blood to the Red Cross. Many women erroneously feel that they are "hemorrhaging" when they lose less than half this amount. Tub baths, douches, and intercourse should be avoided for two weeks following a miscarriage, but other activities can be resumed promptly. The next menstrual period may appear in four to six weeks. It is generally thought to be advisable to wait until after the third menstrual period before trying to conceive again.

Recurrences. If you have aborted before, it may occur to you that another miscarriage will signify there is something terribly wrong with you, that you will never be able to carry a pregnancy to term. Common sense will assure you that this deduction is illogical if you are in good general health. It's like tossing a coin; if you do it long enough, you can toss heads ten times in a row. So don't be discouraged by one, two, or even three miscarriages; or, if you must be discouraged, don't give up.

ECTOPIC PREGNANCIES

As noted in Chapter 2, once in a while a fertilized egg will, in its transit toward the womb, become lodged in the wall of the fallopian tube. This happens once in about 200 pregnancies and it produces an untenable situation. The tubes were not designed to harbor pregnancies. If a fertilized egg does become stuck in the tube it will continue to grow normally for a while; but sooner or later the tube (as opposed to the flexible muscular uterus) will be able to expand its delicate wall no further and it will burst. This in-

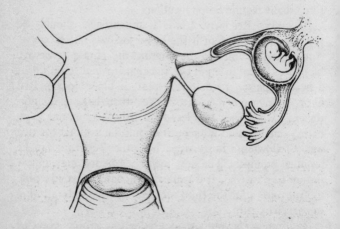

ECTOPIC PREGNANCY. The pregnancy is in the process of bursting through the thin wall of the fallopian tube.

variably happens sooner rather than later—sometime during the first three months. It will produce bleeding directly into the abdominal cavity which must be stopped by an abdominal operation to remove the tube.

Symptoms. Usually the pregnancy seems perfectly normal for a month or two or even three; there are the usual pregnancy symptoms. But there often is some vaginal bleeding, there may be episodes of weakness or actual fainting, and eventually there will be pain, usually on one side of the lower abdomen. These symptoms must be reported to your doctor at once. From here on the matter is in his hands. If he suspects an ectopic pregnancy he will hospitalize you; if his suspicions are confirmed by laboratory tests and ultrasound he will operate immediately. Ectopic pregnancies are medical emergencies of the first order.

Cause. The cause of ectopic pregnancy is not always apparent, though it more often occurs in tubes which have been infected in the past. Many women with a history of ectopic pregnancy proceed to develop future pregnancies in the uterus, where they belong.

MULTIPLE PREGNANCIES

The natural incidence of twins is roughly 1 in 86 pregnancies; of triplets, 1 in 86 times 86; of quadruplets, 1 in 86 times 86 times 86; and so forth. Thus the likelihood of twins, triplets, quadruplets, and quintuplets is approximately 1 in 86; in 7,500; in 650,000; and in 55,000,000 respectively. These ratios have been altered in recent years by the use of drugs in women who do not ovulate spontaneously, which sometimes bring about the extrusion of more than one egg per month. Hence the headlines about quintuplets littering the land. For all practical purposes, however, our discussion can be limited to twins.

Causes and Kinds. Identical twins constitute about one fourth of all twins; there is nothing "hereditary" about them. They occur, as mentioned in Chapter 2, as the result of splitting of the ovum very soon after its implantation in the uterus. The tendency to have fraternal twins is, on the other hand, to a slight degree inherited from either parent. Fraternal twins result from the simultaneous fertilization of two eggs. Except for being born on the same day, they are no more similar than any other pair of siblings. Twin pregnancies tend to occur more often in older women.

Detection. Most pregnant women wonder whether or not they are going to have twins. This is especially true during second and subsequent pregnancies, when women feel that they are "so much bigger" because their abdominal musculature is weaker and the uterus therefore protrudes farther. This possibility is also constantly on the obstetrician's mind, and he has many ways of detecting twins before they are born. His first suspicion may be based, as early as the second month, on rapid enlargement of the womb. Later on he may be further convinced by feeling two fetuses or hearing two fetal heartbeats. Foolproof diagnosis can be made by X-ray or ultrasonogram. Sonogram, the safer of these two procedures, can detect a multiple pregnancy as early as the sixth week, whereas X-rays are not diagnostic until the fifth month. In any case, suspicion must precede diagnosis, and sometimes the obstetrician does not become suspicious until late in the course of pregnancy or even until after the first baby is born.

Care. Twin pregnancies require more meticulous obstetrical care, for complications of many varieties are more apt to develop. The prospective mother of twins will have to be more scrupulous in her diet and in her attention to all of the doctor's advice. She will probably feel doubly uncomfortable during the last few months and will need a great deal of rest. Labor usually occurs two to four weeks before term, but neither labor nor delivery should be unduly difficult. Ironically, if labor begins or the membranes rupture before the thirty-fifth week, a cesarean will probably be performed, to protect these fragile "premies" from the trauma of being squeezed through the birth canal.

One of the most important aspects of a twin pregnancy

is preparation for twin motherhood. It is almost imperative, whether these are the first babies or not, to have help
in the early rearing of them—as much help as you can get.

GERMAN MEASLES

As mentioned in Chapter 4, a woman who develops German measles (rubella) during the first three months of
pregnancy may deliver a deformed baby. This observation
was first made in Australia in 1941 and it has been subse-
quently confirmed many times. The reason for this lies in
the facts that the major body organs (the heart, the brain,
the eyes, and so forth) are formed during the first few
months of life, and the German measles virus can reach
the embryo and affect its development at this time. Cata-
racts, heart anomalies, deaf-mutism, and underdevelop-
ment of the brain may result.

If German measles does occur during the first three
months the odds of a deformity's developing are roughly
one in five. During the fourth month the odds drop to
about one in twelve. After this the chances of the infant's
being affected are practically zero. There is, of course, no
risk to the mother, and regular measles and other virus diseases are not known to cause fetal deformities at all.

During your first visit to the doctor, he probably took
blood from your arm in order to determine your level of
immunity to German measles. If this test shows that you
are not immune (because you have never had the disease
or been vaccinated against it), you cannot be vaccinated
during pregnancy, so you should be extra careful, during
the first four months, to avoid exposure to an active case,
and you should be vaccinated in the hospital after the
baby is born. In some states this is mandatory. If you are
not immune and you are exposed to a case of German
measles during the first half of your pregnancy, a second
blood test will show whether or not you develop the disease.
And if you do develop the disease you will want to discuss

the situation thoroughly with your husband and your obstetrician. There should be no obstacle to your having an abortion in this circumstance if you want one.

THE HAZARDS OF X-RAY AND ULTRASOUND

X-ray. Since the first atom bomb explosion there has been a gradual fallout of facts and rumors about the hazards of all forms of radiation, including diagnostic X-ray. The pregnant woman has been a particular victim in this regard—so much so that an occasional obstetrical patient actually balks these days at her doctor's recommendation that she have X-rays taken to determine the adequacy of her pelvis (X-ray pelvimetry).

It is thought by some investigators that there may be a slightly greater risk of your baby's developing leukemia if your pelvis is X-rayed during pregnancy. Even if this is true the risk is very small—much smaller than the proven risk of injury to your baby if X-rays are not performed when some obstetrical difficulty is suspected.

It is also rumored that X-rays during pregnancy can cause deformities of the fetus. Despite keen concern about this on the part of the medical profession, there is no proof of this. It is possible, if not probable, that excessive radiation during pregnancy may lead to a genetic disturbance which will become manifest by deformities in future generations, 50 or 150 years from now, but the likelihood of this is very small. Doctors are generally ordering fewer X-rays nowadays on pregnant and nonpregnant patients alike, and radiologists are striving to develop more perfect techniques. But there are many sources of radiation other than diagnostic X-rays. The ground we walk on, the air we breathe, and the milk we drink all contain sources of radiation which are equally "dangerous." X-rays comprise but a fraction of the radiation we receive during our lives.

Conclusion: If your doctor thinks that X-rays are necessary in your case, take his advice and don't worry about it.

Ultrasound. High-frequency ultrasonic waves can be used for many of the same purposes as old-fashioned X-rays —and for many new, additional purposes. They may be used to produce a picture (a sonogram) of the uterus and its contents in order to (1) diagnose pregnancy, (2) identify twins, (3) measure fetal size and growth, and (4) detect abnormalities. Used in this way they are harmless.

Combined with a sensor which detects changes in the frequency of these waves caused by pumping of the fetal heart, this technique can also be used to produce audible and visible recordings of the fetal heartbeat. When employed as a brief procedure in the office or labor room there is no harm to the fetus or the mother. When employed continuously during labor (i.e., for periods of ten hours or more), to monitor fetal well-being, it is not known whether the fetus is affected.

MALFORMATION OF THE BABY

The most universal fear of pregnant women is that their babies will be abnormal; the most common question asked immediately after delivery is "Is it all right?" This is a perfectly normal attitude. The fear that nine months of waiting and planning will result in the birth of a deformed baby is certainly natural, as long as this fear is not excessive.

Incidence. In actual fact, however, only one baby in a hundred is severely deformed. This is one statistic which should provide some comfort to the intelligent woman. As mentioned on page 60, most abnormal pregnancies end in miscarriage in the early months. Almost all of the infants that show major degrees of deformity are stillborn—born dead. There are very few instances in which the baby is born alive but badly deformed. Included among these would be cases of neurological (e.g., hydrocephalus and meningomyelocele), intestinal (e.g., tracheoesophageal fistula), and cardiac deformities. Again, if these organ systems are markedly affected the infant usually dies within a few days, although some newer operations have been devised to rectify the less extensive defects of this type.

An intermediate group may be born with afflictions which do not become manifest until later in life, such as cerebral palsy, cystic kidneys, and some forms of congenital heart disease. These are also very rare, and there is new hope in the prevention and treatment of many of these conditions.

The vast majority of congenital abnormalities are relatively minor and correctable. The plastic surgeon can work miracles in reconstructing harelips and cleft palates. Clubfeet can usually be treated successfully without surgery. Undescended testicles, umbilical hernias, and extra digits are among the most common deformities and among the easiest to fix.

Prenatal Diagnosis. Techniques have been developed to detect, before birth, the presence of certain diseases in the fetus. In general this entails amniocentesis, which means inserting a needle through the abdominal wall and into the uterine cavity, removing some of the amniotic fluid, and examining the fetal cells in this fluid for evidence of chromosomal or biochemical abnormalities. Amniocentesis is a simple, almost painless procedure which nevertheless should be done with care, by a specialist, in a hospital setting. A sonogram must be performed immediately prior to the tap itself in order to pinpoint the position of the fetus and placenta. With these precautions, the risk of injury to the pregnancy is less than one in two hundred.

These tests may be performed when there is reason to suspect Down's syndrome (mongolism), certain types of anemia and muscular dystrophy, spina bifida, Tay-Sachs disease, and other fetal abnormalities. And this suspicion arises in these three circumstances: (1) there is a history of such a defect in the mother's or the father's family; (2) the woman has previously given birth to a defective child; and (3) the pregnant woman is over thirty-five, when the

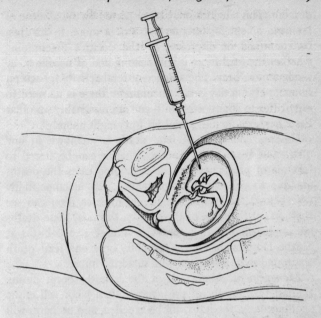

AMNIOCENTESIS. A needle is introduced through the abdominal wall and into the uterine cavity, removing some of the amniotic fluid.

incidence of genetic defects (particularly Down's syndrome) goes up.

If you find yourself in any of these circumstances you will want to talk with your doctor about the desirability of amniocentesis. Usually the test cannot be done before the sixteenth week and it takes an additional two to four weeks to get a report. If the report shows that your baby will be abnormal, you may want to consider having an abortion.

DEATH OF THE FETUS

About one pregnancy in a hundred is complicated by death of the fetus between the fifth month and the onset of labor. This situation may be suspected by the absence of fetal movement for forty-eight hours or more. It can then be confirmed or disproved by the doctor's determining whether the fetal heart is still beating and, if necessary, by sonogram or X-ray. The absence of fetal activity for several hours or even a day is not uncommon; there is no need to report this to your doctor until you are reasonably sure that there has been no movement for forty-eight hours.

Causes. The cause of fetal death is unknown in one quarter of these cases. Another quarter can be traced to toxemia of pregnancy. In the remaining cases the deaths are due to congenital abnormalities, Rh incompatibility (see below), and various maternal diseases. You can see that, except for some of the cases of toxemia, these deaths are unpreventable. In a review of almost 35,000 births at Sloane Hospital in New York City, only one fetal death was found to be associated with maternal injury.

Management. Almost all of these deaths occur during the last two months of pregnancy. Often labor will ensue spontaneously, the fetus will be expelled, and no harm will befall the mother. If labor does not ensue, its artificial induction will be considered by the obstetrician because delay in delivery may result in damage to the mother's blood-clotting mechanism.

THE RH FACTOR

In 1940 a new substance was discovered in the red blood cells of rhesus monkeys. As a tribute to this species of monkey the substance was named the Rh factor. In the course of testing human beings for the presence of the Rh factor, it was learned that 85 percent of us have it and 15 percent do not. Those who have this Rh factor in their red blood cells are called Rh-positive; those who do not are referred to as Rh-negative.

Mechanism of Trouble. If the red blood cells of an Rh-positive person are introduced into the bloodstream of an

Rh-negative person, they will cause the formation of substances known as antibodies which, in turn, will destroy these alien Rh-positive cells. When this happens—i.e., when Rh antibodies form in a person's bloodstream—that person is said to be "sensitized" to the Rh factor. The introduction of Rh-positive blood cells into the bloodstream of an Rh-negative individual can be effected in two ways: blood transfusion or pregnancy. Prior to the administration of a blood transfusion nowadays, the blood cells of both donor and recipient are tested for the Rh factor, and Rh-positive blood is never given to an Rh-negative patient. But in the case of some pregnancies this admixture of Rh-positive and Rh-negative blood is unpreventable. Here is what happens:

In 87 percent of marriages either both partners are Rh-negative, both are Rh-positive, or the wife is positive and the husband negative; no sort of Rh trouble can ever result from any of these combinations. In 13 percent of marriages, however, the wife is Rh-negative and the husband Rh-positive; it is this small group which we are about to discuss, for it is in this group that Rh trouble may develop. In order to understand how it develops, it is important to remember that in most of the cases in which the mother is negative and the father positive (or, for that matter, in the event that either or both of the parents are Rh-positive) the child will be Rh-positive. And in these cases the red blood cells of the baby may, at the time of delivery, enter the bloodstream of the Rh-negative woman and cause the formation of antibodies. The mother is then said to be "sensitized" to the Rh factor. The risk of sensitization is about 15 percent each time such a mother gives birth to an Rh-positive child. When sensitization occurs, the mother's antibodies may then leak into the bloodstream of her babies during subsequent pregnancies, where they can destroy the babies' red blood cells. The first Rh-positive baby in such a setup is invariably unaffected, since sensitization of the mother occurs after she delivers. It is important to realize that the mother, whose red cells are Rh-negative, cannot be harmed by these antibodies, which attack only Rh-positive cells.

Prediction of Trouble. On your first visit to the obstetrician he will take a specimen of your blood in order to determine whether you are Rh-positive or -negative. If you are positive, you have nothing to worry about. If you are negative he will then take a sample of your husband's blood, and if it is also negative you have nothing to worry about. But if your marriage is one of the 13 percent which consists of an Rh-negative woman and an Rh-positive man, it is known in the medical world as an "Rh-incompatible" marriage. In these cases your obstetrician will be alert to the possibility of Rh trouble.

The Prevention of Trouble. Until 1965 there was no way of preventing Rh trouble from developing in a certain percentage of Rh-incompatible couples. Nowadays, Rh sensitization can almost always be prevented by the administration of a sort of anti-antibody drug. Usually known as RhoGAM, when given to a woman within a few days after delivery it will prevent the formation of antibodies which might otherwise affect her next child. (Doctors usually take the extra precaution of administering RhoGAM at the twenty-eighth week, before sensitization occurs, in order to reduce even further any chance of trouble.) This injection must then be repeated after each pregnancy in order to perpetuate this protection.

If you are Rh-negative and your husband Rh-positive I would like to offer this perhaps strange but potentially significant piece of advice: Remind your doctor of this fact after you deliver, so that he will be sure to give you RhoGAM. Although I do not generally advocate patients telling their doctor what to do, doctors' memories are not infallible and in this instance a tactful reminder might prevent a serious problem for you.

It is important to remember, incidentally, that Rh sensitization may occur after an induced abortion, a miscarriage, or even amniocentesis, as well as after a delivery, and that RhoGAM must therefore be given in all of these circumstances.

Treatment of Trouble. If you have already been sensitized to the Rh factor, there is no way of destroying the Rh antibodies that have already formed in your bloodstream and thereby preventing future trouble. The doctor can detect the intensity of this sensitization process, which tends to increase with each succeeding pregnancy, by testing the concentration of antibodies in your blood and, if necessary, in your amniotic fluid (by amniocentesis). And if this antibody level becomes dangerously high he may advise induction of labor three or four weeks before term. As you can see, the management of the pregnancies of Rh-sensitized women is complicated. Such pregnancies should therefore be supervised by doctors who specialize in handling such problems.

Effect upon the Baby. The disease with which these infants may be afflicted is known as erythroblastosis fetalis. It can take several forms. In the milder cases the baby may become a little jaundiced for several days after birth without any lasting effects. If this jaundice deepens, however, it may indicate that a greater number of the baby's blood cells are being destroyed by antibodies, and in such cases the pediatrician may perform what is known as an exchange transfusion, by which the baby's blood is actually replaced with blood which is free of antibodies. A rather remarkable degree of success can now be claimed for this treatment of a disease process which, in days prior to this technique, was often fatal. In the occasional extremely severe case the baby is born dead. If the baby is born alive and properly treated there should be no lasting ill effects.

ABO Incompatibility. Erythroblastosis may also be caused by incompatibility between the infant's and the mother's major blood types. In these cases the baby's blood group is usually A or B, the mother's group O. The mechanism of trouble developing is the same as with Rh trouble: maternal antibodies enter the fetus's circulation and destroy its red blood cells. Although as common as erythroblastosis due to the Rh factor, this type of erythroblastosis has been publicized far less. The reason for this is that the effect upon the infant is rarely serious or permanent, and so this condition is less to be feared. In contrast to Rh trouble, ABO trouble may develop in a first pregnancy. The treatment is the same as that described for erythroblastosis due to Rh incompatibility.

TOXEMIA OF PREGNANCY

Signs and Symptoms. Toxemia is a disease specific to pregnancy which affects primarily the health of the mother, secondarily that of the fetus. It is a disease which occurs only in the last three months of pregnancy and is characterized chiefly by edema (puffiness of the skin, most noticeable around the ankles, hands, and face), high blood pressure, and protein in the urine. Notice that edema is the only one of these cardinal criteria which can be recognized by the patient herself, and of course many women have swollen ankles without having toxemia. This fact serves to emphasize one of the most significant features of this disease: namely, that its onset is insidious and it may develop without the patient's suspecting that anything is wrong. There are other symptoms, such as dizziness, double vision, abdominal pain, headaches, and spots before the eyes, but these are not invariable and not always indicative of toxemia.

Detection. The detection of toxemia obviously then must depend upon the findings of your doctor at the time of your office visits. This is indeed one of the most important reasons for these visits and it explains why the blood pressure, urine, and weight are checked every time. This is why you are asked to report to your doctor any severe headaches, any sudden gain in weight, and any swelling of the hands or feet. For toxemia develops slowly and, like so many other diseases, it can be treated with optimal results if the treatment is instituted before the process has become advanced. If, for example, a woman's blood pressure increases from 120 to 140, the toxemia can usually be corrected; if this early rise goes undetected until the blood pressure reaches 180 or 200, however, the disease process becomes more difficult to reverse and the health of the mother and fetus is in jeopardy.

Causes. The cause of this disease is unknown. Dietary, hormonal, and psychological factors have been implicated. It is known that toxemia occurs more often in women with hypertension, with diabetes, and with twin pregnancies. And, perhaps most important, we know that it occurs much less often among intelligent, cooperative women who have adequate obstetrical care. In some of our southern states, for example, where prenatal care is often lacking, the incidence of toxemia is several times its incidence in other states where care is more uniformly available.

Implications. And what are the implications of toxemia once it develops? In general the gravity of the situation is directly proportional to the severity of the disease. The type of toxemia described thus far is known as preeclampsia; it almost never has any lasting effect upon the mother, but it may occasionally kill the fetus. And if preeclampsia progresses far enough it becomes eclampsia, which is characterized by all of the above symptoms plus convulsions, coma, and/or death of the mother and a high mortality rate among the babies. Fortunately eclampsia is exceedingly rare among obstetrical cases which are sensibly supervised.

Prevention. It is known that women who gain excessive amounts of weight during pregnancy are somewhat more likely to develop toxemia. Hence the importance of diet during pregnancy. You can appreciate the extent to which the prevention of toxemia is emphasized in American obstetrics now that you realize that much of the rationale for dietary regulation, salt restriction, and antepartum office visits is predicated upon this issue.

Treatment. The treatment of toxemia is largely empirical. Bed rest, sedatives, a low-salt diet, and drugs which lower the blood pressure may be used. The only sure cure is delivery of the baby. But let me repeat once more that the most effective form of treatment is prevention, and much of this prevention depends upon you.

MATERNAL DISEASES

Women are no more or less inclined to become ill during pregnancy than they were before pregnancy. Various long-standing and acute illnesses may precede pregnancy or develop during pregnancy. Most chronic conditions such as heart disease and diabetes have an adverse effect upon pregnancy and vice versa. For this reason it is imperative that women with such afflictions seek the most competent obstetrical care they can find as soon as they suspect that they are pregnant.

Urinary Tract Infection. The most common site of infection during pregnancy is the urinary tract—the bladder and kidneys. Characterized chiefly by fever, discomfort in the flanks, frequency of urination, and a burning sensation upon voiding, these infections can be recurrent, especially in women who have had episodes of kidney or bladder trouble in the past. It may sound like a trivial piece of advice but many of these infections could probably be prevented by better toilet hygiene. After a bowel movement it is advisable to wipe the anal area in a front-to-back direction, for bacteria can be propelled toward the bladder by the opposite motion.

Anemia. Anemia is so common among pregnant women that a certain degree of it is to be expected. The hemoglobin values in pregnancy rarely exceed 80 percent of the normal nonpregnant level. But this type of anemia is, in a sense, more apparent than real. That is to say, the standard tests for hemoglobin reveal low values during pregnancy because of the dilution of the blood by increased retention of body fluids. Whatever actual reduction there is in body hemoglobin may be due to the use of maternal iron by the fetus, but this can be counteracted by the adequate ingestion of iron through the diet and prenatal capsules. Cases of pathological anemia, such as pernicious anemia, are rare in pregnancy.

Fibroids. Pregnancy is sometimes complicated by benign fibroid tumors of the uterus. They arise in clusters from the wall of the womb and are composed of the same mixture of muscle and fibrous tissue. They may be as small as millet seeds or as large as grapefruits. During pregnancy they are often responsible for abdominal pain. Although rarely incapacitating in severity, this pain may come and go throughout the nine months and nothing definite can be done about it. Tylenol, ice bags, and rest are helpful. Surgical removal of the tumors, if necessary, must await delivery of the baby; often the fibroids shrink postpartum, so that surgery is not required.

MATERNAL DEATHS

This might be a good place to say a word about maternal deaths. Fifty years ago in the United States the maternal mortality rate was about 70 per 10,000 live births. Now it is about one per 10,000. This dramatic improvement has been wrought by (1) the greater specialization of doctors, (2) the modern emphasis on good antepartum care, (3) the increase in proportion of hospital deliveries, and (4) the advances in medicine such as antibiotics, blood banks, and better anesthesia.

Of the maternal deaths that still occur, roughly one third are due to nonobstetrical factors; that is, they are due to diseases such as cancer and heart trouble which antedated the pregnancy. Another third are associated with inadequate obstetrical care. The remainder can be attributed to pregnancy itself. If you are in reasonably good health, therefore, and if you receive good obstetrical care, your chance of dying during pregnancy or delivery is about one in 30,000. This is much smaller than your chance of being killed on the highway during a long trip. One might almost conclude that your chance of surviving the nine months of pregnancy, if properly cared for, are better than your chance of surviving any other nine-month period in your life, for you are constantly under medical supervision.

Even now obstetricians are sometimes cautioned by expectant fathers to "save my wife and disregard the baby" if a crisis arises. There is no need for such advice these days. This sort of crisis no longer arises. And if it did, doctors would instinctively do their utmost to save their patient.

SURGERY DURING PREGNANCY

Conditions which require surgery, such as appendicitis and gallstones, may occur in the pregnant as well as the nonpregnant individual. Most of these conditions are more common in older women, but it would nevertheless be well for you to be aware of the fact that surgery can be performed during pregnancy, just in case.

Acute Appendicitis. Only one woman among 2,000 develops appendicitis during pregnancy. Appendectomy must be performed as soon as the diagnosis is made. Nausea, vomiting, and pain on the right side of the abdomen are the characteristic symptoms. If you have any severe abdominal pain, call your doctor; don't take any medicine on your own—especially not a laxative. If your appendix must be removed, there will be a slightly increased risk of miscarriage or premature labor during the week following the operation, but the vast majority of pregnancies will be completely unharmed.

Ovarian Cysts. Cysts of the ovary are sometimes discovered during the initial pelvic examination performed at the first office visit. It is a normal phenomenon for small cysts to develop on the ovaries of pregnant and nonpregnant women; they are usually of no medical significance and they disappear spontaneously. With cysts the size of an or-

ange or larger, the story is different. These cysts are prone
to cause trouble during pregnancy and must be removed. If
possible it is best to perform this type of surgery during the
middle trimester, when complications are least likely to
occur. The risk of abortion following this type of operation
is not great.

Other Operations. Most other surgical conditions are
too rare to warrant individual discussion, but suffice it to
say that almost any type of surgery can be performed during pregnancy. Even cardiac surgery is being done. Thyroid
operations are sometimes performed. Gallstones and kidney stones are rare, but they can be removed if necessary.

INDUCED ABORTION

It is not likely that many of you who read this book will
want to have an abortion. Unfortunately, however, some
of you will have to consider this alternative if you are faced
with the possibility of giving birth to a defective child. For
this reason I have decided to include a brief description of
the methods used to terminate a pregnancy.

During the first twelve weeks an abortion can be done
"from below"—vaginally—by D and C (dilatation and
curettage) or suction curettage. The cervix is dilated, with
tapered metal rods, in order to permit the introduction of
other instruments into the uterine cavity. The pregnancy is
then removed with a spoon-shaped instrument called a
curette or through a hollow plastic tube attached to a suction pump. These early abortions are simple and safe. They
are usually performed under local anesthesia on an outpatient basis.

Another method, called hysterotomy, can be performed
at any stage of pregnancy. It is simply a miniature cesarean
section. Like a cesarean at term, it means an abdominal
scar, spending about a week in the hospital, and usually
having future babies by the abdominal route. For these
reasons, and since there is a simpler method for late termi-

nations, hysterotomy is rarely done except in conjunction
with a sterilization procedure.

The simpler method for late abortions is called "salting
out." It is usually done between the sixteenth and twentieth weeks. A needle is inserted through the abdominal wall
and into the uterine cavity (amniocentesis), some of the
amniotic fluid is removed, and this fluid is replaced with a
concentrated salt solution. This will cause a miscarriage in
one to three days. The amniocentesis is associated with no
significant discomfort; the miscarriage, however, may be
moderately painful.

A third technique sometimes used to produce a late
abortion involves the use of a hormone called prostaglandin,
which may be administered by mouth or into the uterus or
vagina.

STERILIZATION

Sterilization is not, as the title of this chapter would
imply, a complication of pregnancy, but I want to discuss
it here rather than at the end of the book in order to
emphasize the importance of your deliberating this action
now rather than after you deliver. Many of you will not
ever want to be sterilized. Some of you will reject the idea
now but consider it after having another baby or two. If
you are among those who think that this pregnancy should
be your last, however, you should at least weigh the pros
and cons and discuss them with your husband and your
doctor while you are still pregnant, for the best time for a
woman to be sterilized is immediately after she gives birth.
And some states require that consent for the operation be
signed at least thirty days beforehand. Your husband's permission, incidentally, is not required.

The Alternatives. If you and your husband are determined not to have any more children after this one, by far
the most certain means of achieving this end is sterilization. But of course this can mean your sterilization or

his. It may be argued that sterilizing the woman is more rational because it is the woman who gets pregnant. And it can be argued that it is more sensible to sterilize the man since the procedure to sterilize him (see below) is far simpler. The only alternatives to male and female sterilization, if you want no more children, are abstinence and contraception until your change of life.

The Pros. The obvious advantages of sterilization, then, are that it is permanent and effective (about one failure in two hundred cases) and that it is far simpler than taking the Pill or using an I.U.D. or a diaphragm for another ten or twenty years. When performed within forty-eight hours of delivery (the optimum time), the operation entails little additional discomfort or inconvenience. There are no subsequent side effects such as interference with menstruation or diminution of libido.

The Cons. The very permanence of sterilization that is so eagerly sought by some women has proven to be its ultimate drawback. For it is often impossible to predict how one will feel about future childbearing. You may change your mind. One of your children may die. Your marriage may break up and you may want to have children by your second husband. All remote possibilities, but they warrant serious thought. Then, too, there are women who, although determined not to conceive again, want to retain this option—just in case. Perhaps it makes them feel more feminine to know that they can get pregnant, even though they don't want to.

The Reasons. By far the most common reason for requesting sterilization is simply to limit the size of the family. Sometimes medical factors come into play. Women with diabetes, heart disease, hypertension, and other conditions affecting their health and that of their offspring may find it wise to stop after one or two children. And women whose babies are born by cesarean should usually be limited to three because of the repeated danger of rupture of the uterine scar.

The Methods. If your baby is born by cesarean and you

want to be sterilized, the delivery and the sterilizing procedure are done through the same abdominal incision. Sterilization following vaginal deliveries entails a separate abdominal operation, leaving a two- or three-inch scar. It is
done within forty-eight hours of delivery. It is technically a
little easier to do this operation a day or two after birth

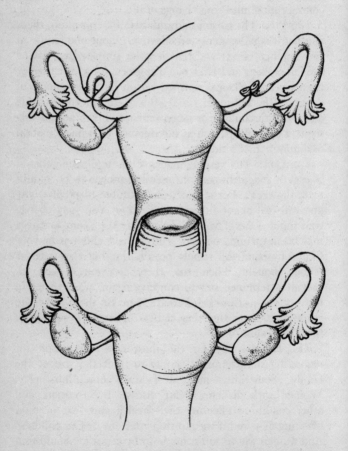

STERILIZATION. A portion of each fallopian tube is tied with catgut
(above, left) and excised (above, right). In a few weeks the catgut
dissolves (below) and the tubes are scarred shut.

than, say, a week or a month later; and of course if it is done at this time it spares the patient another hospitalization.

Since the procedure is known colloquially as "tying the tubes," I imagine that there are many misconceptions of what is done. Actually it is very simple. A one-inch segment of each tube is excised and the cut ends are tied with a catgut suture. Eventually these cut ends become scarred shut, so that the sperm and the egg cannot get together. Sterilization also results from removal of the uterus, tubes, and/or ovaries, but these operations are generally done to treat a specific disease.

Interval sterilizations—i.e., those performed at a time other than immediately postpartum—can be done by the operation described above, through an abdominal or vaginal approach. Or they can be done through a laparoscope —a metal tube inserted through the abdominal wall. Through this instrument the tubes are seen and cauterized —that is, sealed shut by heat. The advantages of the laparoscopic method are a smaller scar (one that can be covered by a Band-Aid) and a shorter hospital stay (overnight or only six to eight hours in an outpatient unit).

In the case of the man, the procedure is known as vasectomy, for it entails the excision of a small segment of each vas deferens—the tiny tube which carries sperm from the testicle. This can be done in the office, under local anesthesia. More and more men are now willing to undergo vasectomy. Of the 1,000,000 sterilizations done in the United States every year, roughly half are performed on men.

6

Normal Labor and Delivery

THE DURATION OF PREGNANCY

At the time of a woman's first visit to the obstetrician, she is given a date when the baby is "due." This is known in medical parlance as "the estimated date of confinement." It is calculated by subtracting three months from the date of onset of the last normal menstrual period and adding one year and a week. If his patient's last period started on July 10, for example, the doctor would subtract three months (April 10), add a year and a week, and tell her that her due date is next April 17.

These dates are at best only rough calculations. Generally speaking, any birth which occurs as much as two weeks before or two weeks after the due date is regarded as a term birth. Only about one in twenty-five term births occurs precisely on the due date; at least a third occur more than ten days before or after.

It is understandable that pregnant women become increasingly anxious, during the last few weeks, to see what sort of baby they have been incubating for so long. But these last weeks are going to be unnecessarily trying for those who count on having their baby on the exact day that it is theoretically due. Greater peace of mind will be achieved by those who convince themselves that the baby is going to be late and are happily surprised if labor starts less than two weeks beyond their due date.

Prematurity. If delivery takes place more than four weeks before term (or, more precisely, if the baby weighs less than five and a half pounds), the baby will be premature. Needless to say, the closer the delivery is to term, the better are the baby's chances. Infants have been known to survive weighing as little as one pound, but this is extremely rare. As a matter of fact prematurity is the greatest single cause of infant mortality today.

Postmaturity. If, on the other hand, labor fails to start within two weeks after the due date, the baby will be regarded as "overdue" or "postmature." Here the accuracy of the date of the last menstrual period is critically important, since the end of a pregnancy is predicted from the date of its beginning. When the duration of a pregnancy does pass the forty-second week, there is an increasing risk that the baby will be adversely affected. A variety of tests have been devised to evaluate the condition of these overdue fetuses. On the basis of such tests and his clinical acumen your obstetrician may suggest that your labor be induced in order to maximize the baby's chances.

Fortunately the vast majority of pregnancies do terminate at term, and so the problems of prematurity and postmaturity need not concern most of you.

PREMONITORY SENSATIONS

Lightening. Lightening is the term used to denote the dropping of the baby's head into the pelvis. With first pregnancies this is apt to occur sometime during the last few weeks. As the fetus descends, the entire womb and waistline seem lower, breathing is easier, and the feeling of enormity is diminished. Concurrently, however, there may be a feeling of increased pressure within the pelvis itself, a desire to void more frequently, and an exaggeration of the waddling pregnancy gait. This dropping is a gradual process, like everything else in Nature, so don't expect a sudden thud. The word is "lightening," as in loads, not "lightning," as in rainstorms. With subsequent pregnancies lightening may not occur before the onset of labor; by then the abdominal wall is usually so lax that any extra room the fetus needs may be found in a forward rather than a downward direction.

False Labor. Also during the last few weeks you are apt to notice that your uterus becomes quite firm every once in a while, although there is no discomfort associated with this change. This firmness signifies that the uterus is contracting. If you are unusually sensitive to pain, you may interpret this process as labor. More accurately, it should be considered "false labor" unless regular contractions ensue at intervals of five minutes or less. The uterus contracts at irregular intervals throughout pregnancy, but since there is rarely any discomfort associated with these contractions until they develop into true labor, they usually pass unobserved. These contractions toward the end of pregnancy serve a definite purpose in softening the cervix and making it ready for the ultimate labor process.

CAUSES OF THE ONSET OF LABOR

Why does a uterus which has harbored a pregnancy for nine months suddenly begin to contract and expel its contents? The simple truth of the matter is that no one knows the exact answer to this puzzle. We have identified most of the parts of the puzzle, but we have yet to discover the magic formula which will enable us to put the pieces together properly.

Hormones. We know, first of all, that there is a hormone secreted by the pituitary gland (the oxytocic hormone) which is in some way involved in the onset of labor. It is usually called Pitocin, and we can bring on labor artificially by giving it to pregnant patients who are at term. But we don't know definitely what triggers the secretion of this hormone by the pituitary.

Distention of Uterus. Secondly, we know that the onset of labor is somehow related to distention of the uterus. When the uterus is distended to a certain point by its contents, it reacts by beginning to contract in order to expel these contents. This is probably why, for example, multiple pregnancies generally terminate spontaneously in advance of term. But why, then, does labor sometimes start in the sixth or seventh month, when the fetus is quite small? No one knows.

Rupture of Membranes. A third known factor which often causes labor to start is rupture of the membranes—colloquially referred to as "the water breaking" or "the bag breaking." This usually occurs at term, but it can occur at any time. No matter when it happens, the escape of water from the womb causes the uterus to diminish suddenly in size and this is usually sufficient to initiate the labor process (see Chapter 7).

Other Factors. There are many other minor factors which are to varying degrees involved in this complex process. The size of the pelvis, the consistency of the cervix, and the presentation of the fetus (whether by vertex or breech) may all play a part, more in some cases than in others. There are occasional patients who have what is known as an incompetent cervix—that is, a cervix which is too weak to retain a pregnancy until term. In these cases every pregnancy may result in miscarriage or premature delivery until the defect in the cervix is repaired surgically.

THE PHYSIOLOGY OF LABOR

The basic concept of what labor is and how it brings about delivery of the baby is not too difficult to understand. And, generally speaking, the better a patient understands it the less she is afraid of the whole process and,

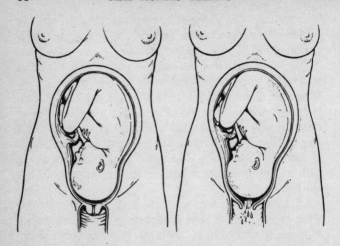

LABOR. The cervix becomes thinner and more dilated as labor progresses. The membranes rupture in the second drawing. The baby's head molds to the shape of the pelvis and gradually descends

hence, the easier her labor is apt to be. This is one of the fundamental tenets of natural childbirth.

The Uterus During Pregnancy. For practical purposes the uterus may be regarded as being composed of two distinct parts: the fundus, which contains the products of conception, and the cervix, which prior to labor prevents the fetus from descending into the vagina. It is the fundus, composed principally of muscle tissue, which contracts rhythmically during labor and thereby pushes the baby down through the birth canal. The cervix, on the other hand, is composed predominantly of elastic tissue which is incapable of contracting. Throughout pregnancy the cervical canal remains tightly closed; during labor it begins to dilate as the baby's head is pushed down through it. This dilatation is accomplished by the action of the fundus, which pulls the cervix up and over the baby's head.

The Uterus During Labor. Hence for nine months the fundus plays a passive role, permitting itself to be dis-

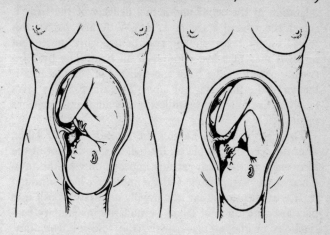

in the birth canal. Following the fourth drawing, the head will continue to descend and, as it does so, it will rotate slowly until it faces backward, toward the mother's rectum.

tended by the growth of the fetus, whereas at the same time the cervix plays the comparatively active role of resisting the pull of gravity upon the fetus and thereby preventing its untimely descent into the vagina. During labor these roles become reversed; it is the fundus which actively contracts and the cervix which passively permits its canal to become dilated. The pregnant uterus can be compared to a balloon which has been filled with water and then tied at its neck. When the tie is broken the walls of the balloon contract and force the water out.

The Stages of Labor. When the cervix becomes completely dilated, it no longer provides an obstacle to further descent of the baby. The cavities of the uterus and the vagina are now continuous. The interval between the onset of labor and full dilatation of the cervix is known as the first stage of labor. With first babies this stage usually takes from six to eighteen hours; with subsequent babies it may take only two to six hours. The interval between full dilatation of the cervix and actual delivery of the baby is called the second stage of labor. With first babies this stage usually takes one or two hours; with subsequent births it may take five minutes or an hour. The time between delivery of the baby and delivery of the placenta is known as the third stage of labor. This stage usually takes less than five minutes, regardless of the number of previous pregnancies.

The Second Stage. During the second stage of labor, after the cervix is completely dilated, further descent of the baby through the birth canal is impeded only by the resistance of the vagina itself and the muscles which surround it. It is at this stage that it is usually necessary to call into play a second force of labor, beyond the involuntary contractions of the uterus—namely, the forceful, voluntary, bearing-down efforts which the patient can exert by tightening her abdominal muscles. Of this, more later.

The Third Stage. As soon as the baby escapes from the uterus the uterus contracts violently, and there is nothing now to prevent these contractions from reducing the size of the uterus itself. Now its only contents are the placenta and membranes, which it promptly tries to expel by continuing to contract. But since these contractions, even when aided by the patient's expulsive efforts, are usually inadequate to effect complete separation and delivery of the afterbirth, the obstetrician almost invariably has to apply pressure upon the fundus through the abdominal wall to terminate the third stage within a reasonable measure of time.

SUBJECTIVE SENSATIONS OF LABOR

Bloody Show. The earliest signs and symptoms of labor are somewhat variable. Oftentimes the very first sign is the passage of some bloody mucus ("bloody show") from the vagina. This signifies the extrusion of the mucous plug from the cervical canal and usually means that labor is imminent.

Rupture of Membranes. Sometimes the onset of labor is heralded by a sudden gush or by a slow leakage of clear fluid (several ounces to a cupful or more) from the vagina, which means that the membranes have ruptured or "the waters have broken." If this happens at any time during pregnancy, you should call your doctor right away. The membranes rupture first in about 10 percent of cases, slightly more often with first babies.

Labor Pains. In the majority of cases the characteristic contractions of labor precede the bloody show or rupture of the membranes. The sensations caused by the contractions may begin with a dull, intermittent low backache, or they may begin with intermittent feelings of discomfort down low in the abdomen, not dissimilar to the cramps many women feel at the time of a menstrual period. These sensations occur at periodic intervals; they last from twenty to forty seconds—never longer than a minute. After a few hours they may disappear or they may become more frequent. When they disappear this is known as false labor and has no special significance. True labor may not begin in these cases for several days or weeks, and during the interim several other episodes of false labor may supervene.

Timing the Pains. If these early, mild, irregular contractions become increasingly frequent and more noticeable, true labor is probably about to begin. It is at this time that you should have your watch handy and actually time the exact interval between the beginning of one contraction and the beginning of the next. Contractions can be recognized either by the discomfort they cause or by the hardening and actual rising up of the uterus which can be felt abdominally by either you or your husband. If you lie on your back you will notice that the uterus becomes tense during a contraction, much as your arm becomes tense when you contract your biceps.

Frequency of Contractions. Sometimes the contractions

begin at regular four- or five-minute intervals. More often they are irregular at first, every ten to thirty minutes; and then, as the interval between them decreases, they become as regular as clockwork—perhaps every fifteen minutes at first, then every ten, every five, and so forth. If you live within an hour of the hospital, your doctor will probably want you either to call him or to go to the hospital when the contractions are coming at about five-minute intervals if it is your first baby—sooner if you have had a baby before. Don't feel, however, that there is any great urgency in your racing to the hospital at this stage, especially if this is your first, for good labor is usually associated with regular contractions every two minutes and, as noted above, the first baby usually takes between six and eighteen hours to arrive.

One important word of advice: once you begin to feel contractions, *do not eat*. You may drink clear fluids, but abstain from solid food.

Arrival at the Hospital. After you have arrived at the hospital, a pelvic examination by the house doctor or the nurse on duty will very promptly tell them how far your labor has progressed. Generally speaking, with first babies the patient is apt to feel that her labor is further along than it actually is, so it is a good policy not to be overly optimistic. If you are, indeed, in early but definite labor, you may or may not be given what is known in labor-room lingo as "a prep and enema." The "prep" consists of shaving some or all of the hair in the genital area, since this hair tends to get in the way while the doctor is repairing the episiotomy. In some hospitals an enema is routine, in others it is optional. Without it, feces are usually expelled with the baby.

Fetal monitoring (see below) may be started soon after your arrival in the labor room. Your husband may join you soon after the prep and enema are given and the monitor is set up.

The Duration of Labor. The duration of the first stage of labor depends on the strength and frequency of your contractions, the size of your baby, the size and shape of your pelvis, the consistency of your cervix, the amount of medication you receive and the timing of its administration, and many other things. Above all, of course, it depends upon whether or not this is your first baby. If it is your first, you are a nullipara (*nullus* meaning none in Latin and *parere* meaning to bring forth) and, as intimated above, the whole process takes about two or three times as long the first time. If a woman's first labor lasts eight hours, for example (and this is about par for the course), her labors with subsequent babies will last in the neighborhood of four hours. And remember that labor begins when the contractions become regular. The early, irregular pains don't count. Your grandmother may tell you that she was in labor for three days. Chances are she is embellishing her story by including a lot of preparatory twinges. Nowadays it is rare for good labor to be permitted to exceed twelve hours.

The Intensity of the Pain. How much pain is associated with labor? In truth, it varies tremendously, for the threshold to the perception of pain varies from individual to individual. There is a small minority of women—some of whom are blessed with extraordinary powers of relaxation or insight or some such magic quality, some of whom have profited to the fullest from a natural-childbirth program— who would say that, although labor is an uncomfortable experience, the pain is far from unbearable and the whole process is so wonderfully miraculous that whatever discomfort they did feel was well worth it and soon forgotten. And undeniably there is another small minority who will tell you that it is the most excruciatingly painful ordeal that one could conceivably experience. But the vast majority, when questioned soon after their babies are born, while the memory is still fresh in their minds, will quite honestly say, yes, it is painful, more so than their modern books on natural childbirth had led them to believe, but certainly less so than the many old wives' tales had implied. And yes, they did feel the need for some medication to take the edge off the pain, but the medication did help and at no time did they suffer unbearably.

It is, I think, unwise to face the prospect of labor with the conviction that it is going to be either painless or unbearable. After all, not even the most ardent natural-childbirth enthusiasts (those who have had a baby, at any rate) claim that childbirth is painless. And obviously labor couldn't be as horrible as some old wives say or there wouldn't be so many mothers so eager to go through it again (and again). If you expect pain without fearing it you will probably not be adversely surprised. Perhaps it is a little like the difference between pinching yourself, which almost never hurts much for you know that this pain stimulus is under your own control, and being pinched by someone else, which almost invariably hurts more, for it is unexpected and out of your control. I have noticed that most women in the midst of labor are both surprised and relieved by the reassurance that their pains will not become perceptibly more severe, for it is natural to expect the worst and this fear does seem in turn to increase the pain. Doesn't the pain caused by a dentist's drill seem more bearable when he informs you that he is almost finished?

The Second Stage. The pains associated with the second stage of labor are a little more severe than those of the first stage—not much, but a little. This is due to the fact that the pain of the first stage is caused almost solely by the stretching of the cervix, whereas in the second stage it is caused by distention of the vagina, a somewhat more sensitive organ. It is at this stage, when the baby's head (or buttocks) descends so far down into the birth canal that it actually presses on the rectum, that most women feel the urge to move their bowels. This is a normal, understandable sensation, for it is caused by the same stimulus which is ordinarily responsible for a bowel movement, namely, pressure on the rectum. And this coincidence is fortunate, for it stimulates the same bearing-down efforts which are associated with a bowel movement and it is these efforts which are essential to the final descent of the baby through the vagina. Sometimes women who do not understand this phenomenon feel that bearing down will cause injury to themselves by overstretching the vagina, but this is obviously not true. If it seems remarkable to you that the vagina can be stretched to such an extent as to permit the delivery of a seven- or eight-pound baby, I can assure you that this never ceases to surprise even doctors who have delivered thousands of babies, and yet it happens, and the vagina is just about the same size after childbirth as before. It might console you to remember that a newborn calf weighs 100 pounds.

Actually the walls of the vagina in its collapsed state, before labor, are pleated, like the sides of an accordion. This explains how the vagina tolerates so much expansion without injury.

LABOR-ROOM ROUTINE

Appearance of the Rooms. Labor rooms vary from hospital to hospital. Some accommodate more than one patient, others are single. Most are sparsely furnished, for reasons of efficiency—a bed, chair, table, and sink constituting the only furniture. Music is often piped in to help you relax. A more homelike setting is provided in so-called birthing rooms, where both labor and delivery take place. And in some private hospitals the patient is left in her own room until her labor is well advanced before she is taken to the labor room.

Examinations. A nurse will visit you at frequent intervals during the beginning of your labor and she will normally stay with you after your labor has become active. It is she who will shave you and give you an enema (if you are to receive a prep and enema), administer your medications, time your contractions, and attend to your needs of the moment. Most labor-room nurses are dedicated souls whose experience, judgment, and empathic powers are

vast. A house physician, bedecked in white, may also check
you occasionally. He may put an intravenous in your arm,
so that medicine can be given to you through the tubing.
Your blood pressure will be checked periodically. The
nurse will listen to your baby's heartbeat with a stethoscope if a fetal monitor is not being used. And pelvic
exams will be done—more frequently as your labor progresses—in order to determine the dilatation of your cervix
and the level of the baby's head in your pelvis. All of
this information will be relayed to your doctor, who will
appear at intervals to examine you. During one of these
exams he may rupture your membranes (if they haven't
ruptured spontaneously)—a painless procedure that speeds
up the labor process.

Fetal Monitoring. Fetal monitoring is routine in some
hospitals, discretionary in others. It may be done continuously, throughout labor, or only at appropriate intervals. This procedure produces a visible tracing (like an
EKG) of both the uterine contractions and the fetal heartbeat and an audible rendition of the heartbeat. There are
two types of fetal monitoring: external and internal. For
external monitoring, two small devices are placed on your
abdomen and held in place with special belts. For internal
monitoring, the fetal heartbeat may be recorded directly
from the baby's scalp (once the membranes have ruptured) or through the mother's abdominal wall, and the
contractions can be recorded from a tube placed in the
uterine cavity. Changes in the fetal heart rate, especially in
its response to the uterine contractions, can indicate fetal
distress, which may be treated by measures as simple as a
change in the mother's position in bed or as drastic as a cesarean section.

Your Appearance. As noted above, you will wear a hospital gown while you are in labor and your jewelry will be
taken from you. Don't plan to have your hair done in preparation for this event. Vanity and modesty are instinctively
shed by the woman in labor. The excitement of experienc-

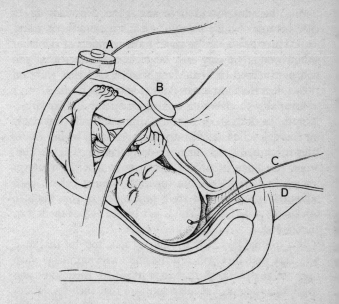

FETAL MONITORING. External monitoring is performed with devices, strapped to the abdominal wall, which record (A) the uterine contractions and (B) the fetal heartbeat. Internal monitoring consists of (C) a device, attached to the baby's scalp, which records the fetal heartbeat and (D) a device, inserted into the uterine cavity, which records the contractions. The doctor will select one of these methods for recording the heartbeat and one for recording the contractions.

ing the miracle of childbirth supersedes the mundane emotions of other-day life.

Your Behavior. Vomiting, defecating, urinating, and bleeding are all, in varying degrees, associated with the labor process. Don't be surprised by them or worried about them. Labor-room personnel are accustomed to these events and they are inexhaustibly prepared to deal with them. If you can't void you will be catheterized. You will not be allowed to eat or drink, for the stomach must be empty in order to prevent the regurgitation of its contents during the administration of anesthesia. No smoking either, because of the proximity of explosive anesthetic gases.

You may be allowed to walk in the corridors of the labor suite if you are in very early labor, but soon thereafter you will be confined to bed. Many women find that lying on their side is the most comfortable position in labor.

Invariably the laboring woman is as fearful of making a fool of herself as she is fearful of the pain itself. Invariably on the day following delivery she apologizes to her obstetrician for her "performance" during labor. This is nonsense. A woman is entitled to behave in labor in whatever manner her spirit tells her to. Most women behave with admirable restraint and stoic pride. But if you want to scream, go right ahead. You won't be the first or the last or the loudest.

It is invariable, too, that women (men, too, for that matter) fear that they will reveal some awful intimacy when they are anesthetized—that they may bare their souls and shock their doctor. Let me assure you that such revelations are never made, and if they were they would not shock the doctor. Before I leave this subject let me warn you that while you may not scream, the lady down the hall may. Brace yourself for this; labor rooms are usually sound-proofed, but no soundproofing system yet devised has met this test.

MEDICATION DURING LABOR

Drugs Commonly Used. Since the first use of morphine in the nineteenth century, a vast variety of drugs has been employed to allay the pain of labor. For many years morphine and scopolamine were used together to produce "twilight sleep," which was much in demand in the 1920s. The combination seemed ideal, for morphine is a very strong narcotic and scopolamine acts with it to produce a dreamy state; but it soon became obvious that morphine was so powerful that, upon entering the bloodstream of the fetus (as most drugs do), it would also narcotize the baby, so that it would be born sluggish and difficult to resuscitate.

In the 1930s, Demerol (a synthetic narcotic) was discovered to have almost the same effect as morphine upon the mother but considerably less effect upon the baby. It soon became the most popular drug for use in labor in this country and it has remained so ever since. Various combinations of Demerol and tranquilizers are most often used. The vast variety of drugs now available for use in obstetrics enables the doctor to choose those which are best suited to the needs of each individual patient. But it must be borne in mind that these drugs, admirable as they are, have at least two main drawbacks. First, if they are given too soon, before labor becomes really well established, they will slow down labor or actually stop it. And, secondly, even these medications must be given in moderation lest they adversely affect the baby. If given in unduly large or oft-repeated doses, they will act upon the respiratory center in the baby's brain and interfere with her ability to breathe after birth. This is especially true of the premature infant, which is apt to be affected by the smallest amounts of medication.

ANESTHESIA

"In sorrow thou shalt bring forth children." Thus did God admonish Eve (Genesis 3:16) and this indeed was the accepted fate of womankind until the discovery of chloroform and ether in the 1840s. So firmly was this philosophy entrenched, in fact, that there were many women and their obstetricians in those days who refused to use these agents in the belief that they were contrary to God's will.

It wasn't long, however, before complete narcosis was the rule in childbirth and women were demanding at least partial narcosis throughout the labor process as well. And now that a whole battery of analgesic and anesthetic drugs have been perfected for this purpose, is it not ironical that the cry is for less and less of them? Sensible as this general tendency may be, there will always be a need for anesthesia in obstetrics and it is important for you to know something about it.

Planning in Advance. There is now such a variety of anesthetics available to the pregnant woman that it has become fashionable, in these days of wanting to know the how and the why of everything, to ask one's obstetrician what anesthetic agents he employs. This is a generally healthy attitude, of course, especially with regard to such matters as ovulation, labor, natural childbirth, and rooming-in, and it is worthwhile learning in advance whether your doctor will grant your wish to be awake or asleep if all goes well during delivery; but this is one sphere of obstetrics which the patient cannot dictate too strongly. Assuming that several types of anesthesia are available at the hospital at which you are going to deliver—and this is usually the case—it is impossible for your doctor to tell you in advance which particular anesthetic will be best for you. So much depends on the size of your baby, the quality of your labor, the size of your pelvis, the possibility of unforeseeable complications, and many other unpredictable factors, that it would not behoove him to promise that you will have such and such a type of anesthesia. Your doctor will surely take your wishes into consideration in making his final decision, but by and large you must realize that this is one matter in which your personal feelings may have to be sacrificed in the best interest of yourself and your baby and in deference to your doctor's judgment.

Gas. Any drug or anesthetic which makes the mother sleepy or puts her to sleep will, after a short while, have a similar effect upon the baby. For this reason ether and chloroform are no longer widely used in obstetrics. These agents have been largely superseded by two types of gas, nitrous oxide and cyclopropane, both of which are faster-acting and therefore safer for the baby. So if you are to be asleep during your delivery, one of these gases will probably be used. Both are pleasant, safe, and free of serious aftereffects.

Pentothal. If you have ever had a minor operation, the chances are that a needle was put into your arm, you were asked to count while a liquid was being injected through the needle, and you were asleep before you counted to ten. Or at least you have probably heard of this type of anesthetic, which is called Pentothal. After Pentothal has been given to induce sleep it is usually supplemented with gas and/or a drug which causes muscle relaxation. These techniques are sometimes used in obstetrics.

Spinal Anesthesia. Spinal anesthesia entails the administration of a solution, similar to or identical with the Novocain used in dentistry, directly into the spinal canal, which is a fluid-filled space surrounding the spinal cord. In obstetrics it is sometimes referred to as "saddle block" anesthesia, since the nerves are blocked from that area of the body which comes in contact with a saddle. It is administered in the delivery room, immediately prior to delivery; it provides immediate, complete relief from pain; and it wears off in about an hour and a half. Stories are rampant that spinal anesthesia is dangerous. It is not—at least no more so than general anesthesia. Headaches can occur following a spinal. They are relieved by lying flat in bed.

Epidural Anesthesia. Epidurals are the same as spinals except that (1) the drug is injected into the space just outside the spinal canal (the epidural area) and (2) it is often given sooner and over a longer period of time. Caudal anesthesia is a type of epidural: a caudal is given into the epidural space through the caudal canal at the base of the spine, whereas other epidurals are given through the space between two vertebrae, higher up on the back. In both cases the anesthetic can be administered during the first stage of labor, after the process is fully established and the cervix is about halfway dilated. The needle may be replaced with a tiny plastic tube through which the anesthetic solution can be periodically replenished, thereby

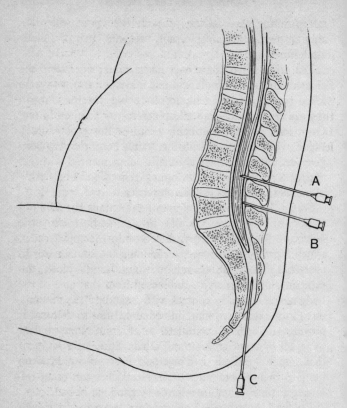

REGIONAL ANESTHESIA. An anesthetic solution may be injected into (A) the spinal canal, (B) the epidural space, or (C) the caudal canal in order to relieve the pain of childbirth.

providing continual pain relief until after delivery of the baby. A continuous caudal or epidural can thus obliterate the worst discomfort of labor while permitting the mother to be fully awake and cooperative and exerting no adverse effect on the baby.

There is a lot to be said for using these techniques in conjunction with or as a substitute for natural childbirth. They cannot be used routinely, however, for a variety of reasons: some women are sensitive to the drug, some labors are too short, some epidural spaces are difficult to tap, some obstetrical situations preclude their use, and some women and/or their doctors prefer other types of anesthesia. In addition, sometimes an epidural gives only partial pain relief or none at all. Fetal monitoring is required with a continuous epidural; together, the anesthesia and the monitor require extra staff, which may not be available. If you like the idea of an epidural, though, you should at least ask your obstetrician if it is available at the hospital where you will be having your baby.

Local. The last type of obstetrical anesthesia in fairly common use today is local anesthesia. Here Novocain or a similar drug is injected just prior to delivery in the area of the vagina, in order to block the nerves which carry pain sensations from the lower pelvis, and/or into the perineum, if you are going to have an episiotomy. All other types of anesthesia are administered by an anesthesiologist. Local anesthesia is given by the obstetrician.

Obstetrical Factors. If used with skill and experience, any one of the above methods of anesthesia is adequate and proper. Some obstetrical situations will demand the use of one type of agent rather than another. It is preferable, for example, to avoid general anesthesia in the delivery of a premature baby; but, on the other hand, it may become mandatory to use a general anesthetic in the delivery of twins. Then, too, it is quite likely that your doctor has worked with certain combinations of drugs and anesthetics that are most familiar to him. He has gained a great deal of experience in his particular methods because he has used them often. For this reason it will be to the advantage of all concerned—you, your baby, and your physician —if you let him use his judgment, his own methods, rather than insist on getting the same anesthetic that your sister's doctor gave her.

THE DELIVERY

The Delivery Room. If this is your first baby you probably will not be wheeled into the delivery room until the baby's head is actually visible at the opening of the vagina. With subsequent pregnancies you will more probably make this move at the end of the first stage of labor. You may be moved in your bed or by stretcher; but at any rate you will ultimately be transferred onto a delivery table. (This paragraph of course pertains only to the conventional labor- and delivery-room setup. If you are having your baby in a birthing room you will remain in bed for the delivery.) Most delivery tables these days are as shiny

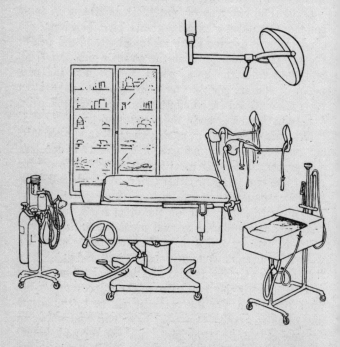

THE DELIVERY ROOM. A slightly simplified drawing in which the stools, basins, bassinet, tables, and instruments have been omitted for the sake of clarity. The mother lies on the delivery table with her buttocks resting on its edge and her legs in the stirrups. An anesthesia machine is seen on the left and a resuscitation apparatus for the baby on the right.

and complex as a modern automobile, each wheel and lever enabling the delivery-room staff to add to your protection and comfort. Overhead there is a small operating room lamp so that the doctor can see what he is doing. And scattered here and there are tables for the doctors' gowns, for the sterile delivery equipment, for the episiotomy instruments; an anesthesia machine; large bowls of antiseptic solution; a bassinet for the baby; a resuscitation apparatus for reviving sleepy infants; stools for the doctors to sit on; and the inevitable glass cabinets full of instruments which look ominous but are rarely used.

Position of the Patient. If you are to have spinal anesthesia, it will be given as soon as you move over to the delivery table. And the next step, regardless of the type of anesthesia you are to receive, is that the nurses put your legs up "in stirrups" and remove or lower the foot of the table so that your buttocks are resting upon the very edge and your legs are up in the air. Until recently your shoulders would have been braced and your hands tied down to limit your movement on the delivery table. Nowadays you will be permitted to move but asked not to touch the "sterile field," in which the doctor must work, in order to protect you from infection.

Preparations for Delivery. While you are being thus positioned on the table your doctor will probably be scrubbing his hands and donning his sterile gown and gloves. He or his assistant will now paint your buttocks and perineal area with an antiseptic solution and perform another pelvic examination in order to determine, among other things, the position of the baby's head. If the baby's head is not down far enough he may ask you to bear down during the next few contractions, during which time you may inhale gas from an anesthesia mask if you so desire. Up until this point you will probably be awake, no matter what type of anesthesia you are going to get.

Delivery of the Head. Now, whether you are having your first baby or your fourth, whether you are to be awake for the delivery or not, the baby is at last ready to be born. If you are to be awake, with caudal, spinal, local, or no anesthesia, it is usually possible for a mirror to be set up so that you can see the entire delivery process. If you are to be put to sleep, now is the time; you will be given an injection or asked to take some deep breaths from a black rubber mask which covers your mouth and nose. At this point the baby's head (or her buttocks) is beginning to "crown"—i.e., it becomes visible at the opening of the vagina when there is a contraction. By now the head has spontaneously rotated or been turned by the doctor so that it faces downward, toward the floor, which makes its delivery easier. When you bear down (as during a bowel movement) with each contraction, more and more of the baby's head can be seen. If you can't push strongly enough the doctor or nurse may help you by exerting manual pressure on your uterus through the abdominal wall. And if this process becomes too prolonged or difficult for your sake or the baby's, the doctor may intervene by delivering the head with forceps or suction. If an episiotomy is necessary it will be done before delivery of the baby's head (see the next section of this chapter).

Women who have little or no anesthesia find delivery of the head the most painful part of having a baby. This pain can of course be diminished by local anesthesia or whiffs of gas inhaled before contractions; and it can be eradicated by an epidural or spinal. Many women find that whatever discomfort they feel is amply counteracted by the thrill of watching their baby emerge from their body.

Forceps and Suction. If you have ever heard of a baby's being permanently scarred or disabled in some way by a forceps delivery, you have probably seen or heard of a baby who was delivered by an incompetent obstetrician. Forceps are no longer used to deliver babies from high up in the birth canal. They are used only to bring the baby's head over the mother's perineum, a maneuver which, if properly performed, will not hurt the baby. It often permits the obstetrician to shorten the second stage of labor by as much as an hour or more, thereby sparing the mother that much

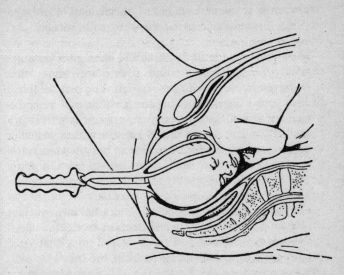

FORCEPS DELIVERY. A cross section of the mother's pelvis, showing forceps applied to the baby's head. By gentle traction upon the handle of the forceps the obstetrician lifts the head out of the birth canal.

pain and preventing a number of spontaneous accidents which might occur to the baby at this crucial stage of the labor process.

Another procedure sometimes used to ease the baby's head out of the birth canal is suction or vacuum extraction. This entails the application to the head of a suction cup or disk which can be pulled by the obstetrician while the mother is pushing during the final contractions.

The Final Moment. After the head is delivered the shoulders are next. Delivery of the shoulders usually requires a further bearing-down effort by the patient or, if she is asleep and unable to bear down, pressure upon the abdomen by the nurse. The body and legs follow spontaneously and at last you can learn whether it's a boy or a girl. Two metal or plastic clamps are placed on the umbilical cord, the cord is cut between the clamps, and the baby is on its own. If you were not given large amounts of analgesic drugs or anesthetic gases, the baby will probably be crying by now.

Seeing the baby for the first time and hearing her cry is a moment you (and your husband, if he is with you) will never forget. Savor it as long as you can. You may be able to hold your baby now or you may have to wait a short while. Try to hold her as soon as you can. It is now that the initial bonding process should begin, a process so vital to motherhood in general and to nursing in particular. You may want to nurse your baby in the delivery room. If you do, the baby will of course get no milk yet, but the sooner you nurse the sooner your milk will come in.

The Baby. The baby will be taken to a bassinet, where any remaining mucus is suctioned from her throat, the umbilical cord is shortened, and she is cleaned up a little. At one and again at five minutes after birth, the baby's condition is measured by the Apgar score. (Virginia Apgar was one of the country's first women anesthesiologists, a leader in her field, and a wonderful human being.) The infant is awarded 0, 1, or 2 points for each of five physical characteristics: color, heart rate, muscle tone, reflex irritability, and respiratory effort. In general, the higher the score, up to a maximum of 10, the better the baby's condition.

Unless you are prepared for it, you may be a little shocked by the appearance of your new baby, for she may be covered with a thick white slippery substance known as vernix, which has much the same consistency as cold cream; she may also be covered with blood from the episiotomy; and her head is apt to have become temporarily elongated in its trip through the birth canal. The vernix and blood are promptly removed and the head returns to its normal shape within a few days. While still in the delivery room, the baby will be identified by wrist band and/or footprint. In the delivery room or nursery her eyes, by law, will be treated with a medicine to prevent gonorrheal infection, which produces blindness. You will have to wait until the baby gets to the nursery before you learn her weight. If there is any problem she will be examined by the house pediatrician.

Delivery of the Placenta. Once the baby is delivered, the third stage of labor is in progress. Within a few minutes usually the placenta has separated from the uterine wall and it is expelled by the obstetrician's applying pressure on the uterus through the abdomen. An injection is now given which causes the uterus to contract further, thereby preventing any unnecessary loss of blood. After the placenta is delivered, don't be surprised if a nurse burrows her hand into your newly flat and flaccid abdominal wall in order to massage the uterus. Although not the most pleasant experience in the world, it is an important measure to assure that the uterus contracts well so that you will not bleed.

Other Types of Delivery. About eighty out of every hundred deliveries follow the above sequence. Breech deliveries and cesarean sections, the principal other types of delivery, are discussed in the next chapter. Twin deliveries occur one at a time, of course, and are not significantly different from other deliveries except that it sometimes becomes necessary to put the mother to sleep in order to extract the second baby. As a matter of fact, twins are usually easier to deliver than single babies because they tend to be smaller. The first delivery I ever did, as a medical student, involved undiagnosed twins and it was as easy as any delivery I have ever done since.

THE EPISIOTOMY

The Rationale. An episiotomy is an incision made at the opening of the vagina just before the delivery of the baby's head. It is usually made with scissors and it may extend for one or two inches onto the skin of the perineum and for the same distance into the vagina. Episiotomies are per-

formed in roughly three quarters of all deliveries in the
United States these days, and the reasons for them are
these: Without an episiotomy the perineum and vagina
often become torn. If these tears are visible they must be
repaired with sutures, and it is easier to repair a clean cut
than a jagged tear. But oftentimes these tears are not visible; they involve only the deep fascia and muscles which
surround the vagina and support the bladder and rectum.
This type of tear cannot be repaired, and the eventual result of such a disruption of these fascial and muscular supports is that the bladder and rectum become loosened
from their normal moorings and protrude into the vagina.
The full effect of these injuries may not become apparent
for many years. You have probably heard of old ladies
whose vaginas turned inside out or who could no longer retain their urine; this is why. The episiotomy is also done to
protect the baby's delicate head from being injured by
undue pressure from the intact perineum; this is especially
true in the case of the doubly delicate head of a premature
infant. So you can see that these incisions protect the
mother and the baby from hidden injuries which might
otherwise occur.

The Method. Episiotomies can be done in two different
ways. The incision may extend in a straight line from the
vagina toward the anus, or it may be curved away from the
anus toward the right or left leg. They are repaired with
catgut sutures (the word "catgut" being a misnomer since
this suture material is actually made from the intestinal
lining of sheep). Within a week or two these sutures dis-
solve and the superficial ones fall out; in other words, they
do not have to be removed. Women often ask how many
stitches were taken, but the answer to this question is
meaningless. The doctor may have taken numerous
stitches with the same piece of thread or he may have
taken a series of individual stitches, some of which may be
in the muscles, some in the skin. The stitches may be close

together or far apart. Furthermore, the doctor is too busy to count them.

THE INDUCTION OF LABOR

When the doctor initiates the labor process rather than waiting for it to begin spontaneously, this is referred to as the induction of labor.

Why It's Done. Until the mid-1970s labor was often induced electively—that is, merely for the convenience of the pregnant woman and her obstetrician. This is uncommon now. Inductions these days are largely restricted to situations in which there is a medical indication, when it seems safer for the mother and the baby to have the baby born than to let the pregnancy continue. Such indications include some cases of diabetes, hypertension, heart disease, toxemia, and other maternal conditions, and threats to the baby's well-being such as postmaturity and Rh sensitization.

When It's Done. During the last week or two of pregnancy, the cervix usually starts to dilate. This dilatation of the cervix is one of the principal indexes by which the obstetrician can tell that labor is imminent. If this dilatation progresses to a sufficient extent (two centimeters or more) and if all other conditions, such as the position of the baby, are propitious, labor can be induced easily. If the cervix has not yet begun to dilate, induction will probably be more difficult and may have to be attempted more than once.

How It's Done. Usually this entails rupture of the membranes (which is often done in the course of spontaneous labor) and the administration of a drug which causes the uterus to contract (the same hormone responsible for the onset of spontaneous labor). This drug, called Pitocin, or "Pit," is added to an infusion of glucose and water and given intravenously. There is often a latent period of half an hour or more when nothing happens. Then the contractions begin. As with spontaneous labor the contractions are apt to be mild and irregular at first. Rupturing the membranes tends to speed up the process.

NATURAL CHILDBIRTH

Natural childbirth is a term coined in the 1940s by Grantly Dick-Read, a British doctor who wrote a book on the subject entitled *Childbirth Without Fear*. It was his observation that women who lose their fear of having a baby will have less pain in labor. And this is generally true. The fear may be lessened by learning what labor is all about—through attending classes, reading books, and talking to your doctor. In addition, natural childbirth entails performing certain exercises during pregnancy and in labor, which help to relax the body, control the muscles, and distract the mind. The doctor, nurse, and husband play important supportive roles through exhortation, encouragement, and massage.

When natural childbirth was first introduced it was regarded by many women as a sort of substitute for modern obstetrical management. They felt impelled to experience the entire labor and delivery process without medication, anesthesia, forceps, or episiotomy. This was unfortunate for two reasons: most women simply cannot succeed in this without considerable pain; and there are definite medical advantages to be derived from modern obstetrical methods. Furthermore, many of the women who needed pain relief, after having been led to believe that they would need none, felt that they had failed, that they had somehow not measured up to the mark of normal, motherly women.

The principles underlying natural childbirth are nonetheless sound—so sound, in fact, that they have been known to the obstetrical profession for a hundred years. The pain of labor is intensified by the tension which results from fear, and hence this pain can be reduced through education and relaxation. But the degree of relief necessarily varies from individual to individual, just as the individual perception of pain varies. Some women have totally painless labors without ever having heard of natural childbirth; others go to all the classes, read all the books, practice all the exercises, and still ask to be put to sleep.

PREPARED CHILDBIRTH

When it became apparent that most women cannot or should not go through labor and delivery without the benefits of modern medicine, the concept of natural childbirth became slightly altered and a more moderate approach was introduced, called prepared childbirth. The basic principles of education and exercise remain the same, but women are not led to believe that these measures will lead to totally painless labor, they are encouraged to ask for medication if they need it, and they are urged to accept their doctor's advice with regard to anesthesia, forceps, and episiotomy.

This compromise has worked very well. As a matter of fact, I have never seen a patient who has not profited from this approach to having a baby. Because these women are "prepared" with regard to what to expect, they are less afraid, they have less pain, and they actually require less than half of the usual amounts of medication. Whenever possible, regional (rather than inhalation) anesthesia is used, so that the patient is wide-awake and able to participate in the delivery. And whenever forceps and/or episiotomy are indicated, the mother and the baby profit from their use.

Some fortunate women, with high pain thresholds and rapid labors, are able to undergo the entire experience without any analgesia or anesthesia, but at least those who can't are not led to believe they have failed. Of course, most of the women in prepared-childbirth programs are about to have their first labor, which is apt to be the most prolonged, so some pain relief is usually in order. Preparation and medication have proved to be a good combination in these cases. At the time of this writing, the cost of prepared-childbirth classes ranges between $50 and $75— for a series of ten classes and one postpartum get-together.

There are several natural-childbirth "schools." The most popular in this country are those associated with the names of Bradley, Harris, Lamaze, and Leboyer. Though the techniques taught by these schools are quite different, the end results are objectively the same. The overall success of natural or prepared childbirth seems to depend far more upon the woman's personality, her pain threshold, and her confidence in the doctor.

The Husband. One of the features of every natural- or prepared-childbirth program is inclusion of the husband. The husband is expected to attend the classes so that he too will learn about the physiology of pregnancy, labor, and delivery. So informed, he is better able to help his wife throughout pregnancy and to stand by her during labor. His mere presence often serves as a source of strength to her and renders the experience a memory which both of them can cherish.

The desire on the part of a wife for her husband to attend her in labor may stem from several sources. Ideally she wants him near during such a supreme moment in their lives. Sometimes she feels that he will bolster her courage if it falters. And occasionally she wants him there to witness her suffering. It is important, therefore, for you to examine your motives in this regard and to be sure that they are straightforward and unselfish. Husbands vary, too, in their desires to share this experience. Many feel adamantly that there is nothing "natural" about their getting into the act at this stage. Surely, they argue, the aboriginal male was never found in the same tent with his laboring spouse. So examine your husband's feelings too. If he is obviously enchanted by the idea, fine; but if he seems at all leery, don't push him.

The husband is expected under these circumstances (1) to help time the labor contractions, (2) to massage his wife's back during contractions, and (3) to provide moral support. If it becomes apparent as labor progresses that he is becoming unexpectedly squeamish, this is the time for true altruism: let him off the hook; let him go home. Most husbands, on the other hand, want to stay on through the delivery itself. And most hospitals permit this. When it is permitted, the husband is expected to don a gown, cap, and mask and to remain at the head of the delivery table. If complications arise, it will be suggested that he leave the room.

Comment. Most women find that the contractions of labor are painful. There is no doubt that this pain is intensified by fear and ignorance. The very fact that you are reading this book demonstrates your healthy desire to dispel this fear and ignorance. Further steps should include (1) choosing an obstetrician you will have confidence in and, if possible, (2) enrolling in a prepared-childbirth class. You will then have done all you can to reduce the discomfort of having your baby. Let your doctor do the rest.

7

Abnormal Labor and Delivery

If all labors and deliveries were perfectly normal there would be little need for obstetricians. Many labors and deliveries are complicated, to varying degrees, and must be skillfully handled. It is important that the pregnant woman be informed about some of these complications, in order that she recognize them if they occur and realize what they portend. It is easier to understand and appreciate normality if we study the abnormal. And it is through cognizance of these problems that women will realize the advantages of being delivered by a good obstetrician at a good hospital.

PREMATURE RUPTURE OF THE MEMBRANES

The membranes rupture spontaneously before the onset of labor in approximately one out of every ten cases. This, of course, can happen at any stage of pregnancy. If it happens at or near term, labor will almost surely ensue within twenty-four or forty-eight hours. This sequence of events is actually favorable, for labor in these cases tends to be slightly shorter than average. If labor does not ensue spontaneously, it will probably be induced by your obstetrician in order to avoid the danger of infection ascending from the vagina into the uterus and thence to the baby.

If, on the other hand, the membranes rupture before term—say, in the sixth or seventh month—a somewhat different situation prevails. The risk to mother and baby of intrauterine infection must be considered, together with the risk to the baby of being born prematurely and of being squeezed, at this tender age, through the birth canal. Because antibiotics are not terribly effective in preventing infection once the membranes have ruptured, because great advances have been made in the care of premature infants, and because it is known that premies fare better after abdominal delivery than after vaginal delivery, cesarean section is often resorted to when the membranes rupture before the thirty-fifth week—whether labor has started or not. Until recently premature infants delivered in this way were subject to serious pulmonary complications, which can now be largely prevented by administering a drug to the mother. This drug, betamethasone, must be given twice, at twenty-four-hour intervals, before the cesarean is performed.

PREMATURE LABOR

The fetus may be expelled by the uterus at any time during pregnancy. If this occurs before the end of the twentieth week it is called an abortus, with no chance of survival; between the twentieth and the twenty-eighth weeks, an immature infant, with a poor chance of survival; between the twenty-eighth and thirty-sixth weeks, a premature infant, with a fair chance; and, after the thirty-sixth week, a term infant, with an excellent chance. One out of ten pregnancies terminates in the premature range.

Causes. In some cases premature labor is precipitated by maternal disease (such as toxemia), by twins, separation of the placenta, or rupture of the membranes. In half of the cases the cause is unknown.

Management. There is no foolproof way to stop premature labor once it is fully established. One essential part of any such treatment is complete bed rest. In addition, there are drugs which are used with varying degrees of success. After the labor process becomes irreversible, special care must be taken not to harm these tiny infants. The use of analgesia and inhalation anesthesia is avoided in an effort to protect the baby from the hazards of narcosis. A certain amount of stoicism is necessary on the part of the mother in labor; spinal, caudal, or local anesthesia may be used for the delivery.

Prognosis. Despite recent gains in our knowledge about the care of premature infants, prematurity remains a leading cause of infant mortality. The survival rate is, as you would expect, directly related to the birth weight. An infant weighing 1,000 to 1,500 grams (about 2 pounds 3 ounces to 3 pounds 5 ounces), for example, has a 60 percent chance of survival, whereas an infant weighing more than 1,500 grams has better than nine chances in ten. In order to maximize these chances for a premie it is essential that the infant be placed in a special premature nursery unit equipped and staffed specifically for the care of these delicate creatures. There the baby will remain until she weighs about 2,500 grams (5½ pounds). And since this may take several weeks the hospital bill may be astronomical. If your baby is placed in such a unit, speak to the hospital's social worker about applying for government aid to pay this bill.

SLOW LABOR

"False" Labor. When a woman says that she was in labor for three or four days, what does this mean? It means, quite simply, that the mother was in false labor for several days before the onset of true labor. No woman is

permitted to remain in real, honest-to-goodness labor for longer than a maximum of twenty-four hours.

Causes. As a matter of fact, it is rare these days for labor to last longer than about twelve hours, even with the first baby. So what is the explanation of labors which go on for twelve to twenty-four hours? There are two main causes for this: (1) There may be an element of disproportion between the size of the fetal head and the size of the maternal pelvis, i.e., the baby may be so large or the pelvis so small (or both) that it takes longer for the baby to be squeezed through the birth canal. Or (2) the contractions of the uterus may be unduly weak, a condition known as uterine inertia.

Treatment. The former problem is discussed below, under the heading "Cephalopelvic Disproportion." If the disproportion proves to be too great, a cesarean section must be done.

In the event of uterine inertia, the management is usually much simpler. The administration of minute amounts of Pitocin, the oxytocic hormone from the pituitary gland, almost invariably enhances the quality of the contractions so that labor is speeded up. In the occasional case where Pitocin fails, a cesarean may have to be resorted to. Other conditions which retard the progress of labor are too rare to mention.

All in all, with the more extensive use of Pitocin and cesarean section, obstetrics has entered an era in which the pregnant woman rightfully expects to have a reasonably short labor, shorter by several hours than her foremothers'. This change has been partly responsible for a decrease in maternal and infant morbidity.

DRY LABOR

The phrase "dry labor" is mentioned only because it has been ingrained in the lay mind. Actually there is no such thing as dry labor. The phrase is meaningless. It has become a widely accepted misconception that if the membranes rupture before labor or early in labor this will have some deleterious effect upon the baby. This is so far from the truth that obstetricians sometimes make a point of rupturing the membranes early in labor in order to speed up the process. There is no effect upon the baby from this practice other than to hasten its transit through the birth canal.

It is known that the membranes constantly produce amniotic fluid at a rate of almost a pint an hour. Even if the membranes rupture a month or more from term, this fluid continues to be produced and to bathe the baby. Hence, no labor is "dry."

CEPHALOPELVIC DISPROPORTION

If the mother's bony pelvis is unusually small or misshapen and the baby is average in size, it may be difficult or impossible to deliver the baby vaginally. If the mother's pelvis is average in size and the baby enormous, the same situation may prevail. This is called fetopelvic or cephalopelvic disproportion. The latter phrase is actually the more precise of the two, for the head (*kephale* in Greek) is the largest and least compressible part of the baby and hence the only part which need be considered in problems of this sort. Despite its relative lack of compressibility, however, the fetal head can and usually does change in shape during the course of labor. By this reversible process, known as molding, the head becomes elongated and its circumference thereby slightly reduced.

Diagnosis. The obstetrician estimates the size and shape of the patient's pelvis during the pelvic exam performed during her very first visit. Then when the pregnancy reaches term he estimates the size of the baby. In the vast majority of cases these estimates will reveal that the pelvis is sufficiently large to permit safe vaginal delivery. In rare cases the discrepancy between fetal and maternal measurements is so extreme that the obstetrician can proceed with a cesarean section before the onset of labor in the knowledge that vaginal delivery is impossible. X-rays must sometimes be taken just before or during labor in order to determine whether disproportion exists. By this technique, known as X-ray pelvimetry, fairly accurate measurements may be taken of both the maternal pelvis and the fetal head.

Trial of Labor. There remains a small number of cases in which this issue cannot be settled without an actual "trial" of labor. If sufficient progress is not made after a reasonable length of time, a cesarean section is performed. It may seem cruel to permit these women to undergo both labor and a cesarean section, but, with first babies especially, this is sometimes the only way of avoiding an unnecessary cesarean. And since cesarean section is still a major operation, one which usually has to be repeated with future pregnancies, there is really no intelligent alternative.

The problem of disproportion is somewhat different when the fetus presents by the breech, for in these cases the head is delivered last and therefore has no chance to mold to the shape of the pelvis. If disproportion is suspected in these cases, cesarean section is usually performed without a trial of labor.

CESAREAN SECTIONS

The origin of the term "cesarean section" is obscure. In the days of the early Roman emperors there was a law referred to as the "lex caesarii" (the law of the emperors), which proclaimed that women who died during pregnancy should be delivered immediately after death by abdominal incision. Such an operation on a living woman was unsafe and unheard of in those days. Quite possibly our term has its origins in this antique proclamation. The more popular belief that Julius Caesar was thus delivered is less tenable for the simple reason that his mother survived his birth.

Indications. A woman's first cesarean section is referred

to as "primary," her second as "secondary," and so on. The majority of primary cesareans are done for cephalopelvic disproportion. Others are done for placenta previa and premature separation of the placenta (which are described below), for uterine inertia, for fetal distress, and for other rare conditions in which there would be greater risk to the mother or baby in vaginal delivery.

"Once a cesarean . . ." Perhaps you have heard the expression, "Once a cesarean, always a cesarean." It is an old obstetrical aphorism meaning that once a woman has a cesarean section, all of her future deliveries will have to be managed in this way. Generally speaking, this is true. There are many reasons for this, the most important of which is this: When a uterus is cut in the course of a cesarean it becomes permanently scarred. This scar will always be weaker than the rest of the uterine wall and so with every subsequent pregnancy there will be a small but definite (about 1 percent) risk that this scar will rupture. Most of these ruptures occur in labor, when the scar is under stress. And since rupture of the uterus usually results in a dead baby and a very sick mother, it is understandable not only that cesareans are repeated but also that they are usually performed a week or two in advance of the due date, before labor is apt to occur.

In recent years the incidence of delivery by cesarean section has risen. In part this has been due to the development of more sensitive techniques (e.g., fetal monitoring) for detecting signs of fetal distress. As more women have undergone cesareans for such reasons, more of them have requested that their future offspring be delivered by the vaginal route. To a degree, this argument makes sense in those cases where the first cesarean was done for an accidental reason, such as fetal distress, rather than for a recurrent reason, such as cephalopelvic disproportion. Again, this is an issue that must be decided on an individual basis. You will find that most good obstetricians are fairly cautious on this score.

Number of Cesareans. Because of this risk of rupture of

the uterus, sterilizations are often performed after two or more cesareans. The risk of rupture seems to be no greater with each succeeding pregnancy, but the patient undergoes this risk each time. Women have been known to have as many as twelve cesarean sections; they have taken twelve small chances of getting into serious trouble.

The Operation. Cesarean sections can be described as the simplest and at the same time the most dramatic of major operations. The abdominal wall is incised, vertically or horizontally, for a distance of about six inches; the uterine wall is incised, usually horizontally, for about the same distance; the baby and placenta are delivered; and the incisions are then sewed up. The whole operation takes about an hour. The main source of concern is hemorrhage, for the pregnant uterus bleeds furiously when it is cut; but this rarely reaches serious proportions and, when it does, it can be counteracted by blood transfusions. Almost any type of anesthesia can be used; spinal and epidural are the most popular because of their lack of effect upon the baby.

The Recovery. Recovery from a cesarean entails a moderate amount of abdominal discomfort for about forty-eight hours, discomfort which is largely dispelled by analgesics. From the third day on, convalescence is rapid; the mother may nurse; the skin sutures are removed after five to seven days; and the patient is usually able to go home and take care of her baby on the fifth or sixth day.

PLACENTA PREVIA

Normally the placenta is attached high up on the interior wall of the uterus. Only once in about 200 cases is it attached low down in the region of the cervix. This latter condition is known as placenta previa, from the Latin word *praevius*, meaning going before. Sometimes the placenta is implanted in such a manner that it entirely covers the cervical canal (central placenta previa); sometimes only the edge of the placenta infringes upon this opening (marginal placenta previa).

The Hazards. Since it is essential that the baby be delivered before her placenta, central placenta previa creates an obstetrically untenable situation which must be managed by cesarean section. The main hazard in these cases is hemorrhage. No matter where the placenta is located, the area of its attachment to the uterus is extremely vascular, for all of the maternal blood vessels nourishing the fetus must congregate there. As the cervix starts to dilate toward the end of the pregnancy, and especially in labor, a placenta attached to the cervix will be gradually torn loose. The combination of vascularity and tearing results in vaginal bleeding.

These simple facts explain at once the symptoms, the dangers, and the principles of diagnosis and management of cases of placenta previa. The one and only symptom is intermittent painless vaginal bleeding in late pregnancy. The danger is that this bleeding will be massive and that it will occur without medical supervision. Fortunately the first episode of bleeding is rarely massive and can serve as a warning to the patient and the doctor.

Management. If painless vaginal bleeding occurs late in pregnancy, an ultrasonogram will be performed to establish the location of the placenta. If the suspicion of placenta previa is confirmed by the sonogram, management of the problem will depend on whether the bleeding is slight or profuse, whether the placenta previa is marginal or central, and whether the fetus is premature or term. A central placenta previa at term would dictate an immediate cesarean section. Other cases will be individualized. Prior to the thirty-seventh week the doctor will probably pursue a "hands-off" policy, giving the fetus every chance to reach term before delivery. If profuse bleeding occurs at any time, his hand may be forced. If labor starts, the method of delivery will depend upon the amount of bleeding, which, in turn, will depend upon whether the labor is fast or slow and whether the placenta previa is central or marginal.

By no means does all late pregnancy bleeding stem from placenta previa. Although all such cases have to be handled with placenta previa in mind, often the source of the bleeding is much more trivial. And even if a placenta previa does exist, all well-trained obstetricians know how to handle it, so the risk to mother and baby is slight.

PREMATURE SEPARATION OF THE PLACENTA

Another cause of bleeding in late pregnancy is premature separation of the placenta. This condition occurs once in about 100 deliveries.

Implications. Normally the placenta separates from the uterus in the third stage of labor, after delivery of the baby. Occasionally this separation begins to take place during the later months of pregnancy, before labor begins. The cause for this is unknown, although it occurs most often in patients with toxemia. Since the placenta is the fetus's sole source of oxygen and food, its premature separation will result in immediate fetal death if it involves a major portion of the placenta's surface. And since the site of attachment of the placenta to the uterus is so very vascular, its detachment will also cause bleeding from the uterus, which usually manifests itself vaginally.

Symptoms. Unlike placenta previa, premature separation of the placenta is characteristically associated with abdominal pain as well as bleeding, and it is soon followed by the onset of labor. In contrast to placenta previa, too, there is but one episode of bleeding, which does not stop until delivery of the baby.

Outlook. In most cases it is just an edge of the placenta which separates, a situation which can be handled conservatively with a good prognosis for successful vaginal delivery. If a large area of placenta is detached, the outlook is less hopeful. In the latter event, timing of the treatment is of the utmost importance to the fate of the baby. Sometimes the timing involves hours, sometimes mere minutes. Cesarean section will be done if the baby is still alive. The risk to the mother is never great, thanks to the modern blood bank.

BREECH PRESENTATION

Of every hundred term deliveries, the back of the baby's head (the vertex) comes first in ninety-five, the baby's buttocks (the breech) comes first in three, and the face, brow,

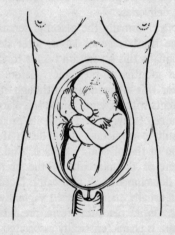

BREECH PRESENTATION. The baby's buttocks will be born first. There will be no opportunity for the baby's head to become molded by the birth canal.

or shoulder leads the way in two. The reason for this preponderance of vertex presentations is simply that this is the position in which the fetus best accommodates itself to the inverted pear shape of the uterus. This is fortunate since the head-first position presents the fewest problems in obstetrical management. Prior to term the incidence of breech presentations is much higher.

The Risks. The risk to the mother from breech delivery is no different from that of vertex delivery, but the risk to the baby is increased threefold. The factors responsible for this greater fetal hazard are several. Since the head is not gradually squeezed through the birth canal, as with vertex presentations, it does not become molded and hence will be more difficult to deliver unless the pelvis is capacious. And since the baby's bottom fits less snugly than its head into the pelvis, there is a greater chance that the umbilical cord will insinuate its way around the fetus and into the vagina, an accident which imperils the fetus's supply of oxygen. The delivery itself is not complicated if the size of the pelvis is adequate.

Management. X-rays of your pelvis will probably be taken if you begin labor with the breech presenting, for it is vitally important to know in advance whether your pelvis is sufficiently large. If it is under average in size, a cesarean section will be done without a trial of labor. Cesareans are much more common with breech presentations.

As I have said several times already, anyone can handle an uncomplicated delivery. And a good obstetrician will know how to handle the unusual situation. In the case of a breech, he will know when to order X-rays and how to interpret them, when to do a cesarean section, and how to deliver the baby vaginally. So if you have a good doctor you have no need to worry about your baby's coming fanny first.

8

Motherhood in the Hospital

Most women who have never had a baby tend to underestimate the importance and complexity of the first month of motherhood. They seem to regard the process of procreation as one which involves (1) being pregnant, (2) being delivered, and (3) raising a baby. But in between the last two stages there lies the crucial phase of transition which entails recovering from stages 1 and 2 and preparation for stage 3. This phase is known in medical parlance as the puerperium. It is in many ways more vital that a woman be well prepared for the puerperium than that she be prepared for the delivery itself. Indeed the delivery can and often does occur with no cooperation whatsoever from the mother; it is after the baby is born that her cooperation becomes completely essential.

Although no one has gotten around to emphasizing the importance of this phase of childbirth to the extent, for example, of referring to it as "puerperium without fear," there has been a commendable resurgence of interest in certain aspects of it, as evidenced by the growing popularity of breast feeding and rooming-in. And there are many other facets to these exciting early weeks of motherhood with which you should be familiar. Read the following words and discuss the issues with your doctor. Without meaning to belittle natural childbirth, I think you will agree that natural motherhood is an even greater goal to strive for.

THE RECOVERY ROOM

After having graduated from the labor room and the delivery room, you may be placed in a third strange environment, the recovery room, where you will spend the first hour or so of your new motherhood in the company of several other young women who have just undergone the same experience. Medically speaking this further hour of observation is an hour well invested, for it is during this interval that an occasional woman will develop a complication, which will be most promptly observed and treated in this, one of the most scrupulously surveyed rooms in the entire hospital. If all has gone well, your husband and your baby may now be with you for an hour of quiet celebration. Take advantage of this interlude to get some rest—before the flowers, the phone calls, and the fanfare.

MINOR ANNOYANCES

Most women expect a certain amount of discomfort during pregnancy and labor, but it usually comes as a surprise to them that there may be some further discomfort associated with the immediate postpartum period. In the average case this discomfort is minimal; it is apt to stem chiefly from the uterus ("afterpains"), the episiotomy, and the breasts. Since it is likely that you will experience some of these sensations, it is well that you be prepared for them.

Afterpains. Afterpains are lower-abdominal cramps, not dissimilar from menstrual cramps, which are due to the continued contractions of the uterus as it strives to shrink down to its nonpregnant size. Immediately after delivery of the baby and the afterbirth the uterus assumes the size of a grapefruit. During the first postpartum week it shrinks further to the size of an orange, and in the ensuing weeks it returns to its normal size, which is about that of a lime. This shrinkage is accomplished by contractions of the uterus, which may be felt as cramps of variable severity during the first two days after delivery. These contractions, which are usually less bothersome after the first delivery, are apt to be intensified by nursing—which actually hastens involution of the uterus and thereby prevents bleeding—and by the tiny white pills which you may be asked to take for a few days. These pills contain Ergotrate, a powerful oxytocic (from the Greek *oxys* meaning swift, and *tokos* meaning birth; this drug is too powerful to be given before birth of the baby) which stimulates the uterus to contract. Afterpains are effectively counteracted by codeine, Tylenol, and other mild analgesics.

Episiotomy Pain. Episiotomy pain is variable. Oftentimes it is negligible, sometimes it is annoying, occasionally it is more than annoying. The degree of pain is determined partly by the location and size of the episiotomy, but by and large it is impossible to explain why some episiotomies hurt more than others. The cause of the pain is that the tissues in this region swell a little and pull against the stitches. This swelling, and hence any discomfort associated with it, usually reaches its peak on about the third postpartum day and then gradually subsides. Healing of the episiotomy is promoted by keeping this area clean and dry. The discomfort is usually relieved by the use of a heat lamp, an anesthetic spray, ice bags, and, again, codeine or Tylenol.

Breast Engorgement. Breast engorgement is an almost universal phenomenon which occurs on the third or fourth postpartum day, when "the milk comes in." Due not to distention of the breasts with milk, but to engorgement of the veins and lymphatic vessels, this condition can cause the breasts to become hard and uncomfortable whether the mother is nursing or not. It subsides spontaneously in a day or two. Simply binding the breasts rather tightly against the chest wall with a breast binder or maternity brassiere is usually sufficient to relieve the discomfort. Ice bags and mild analgesics are also helpful. Some doctors prescribe a drug to prevent lactation in nonnursing mothers. To be effective, this drug should be given immediately after birth, so make sure your obstetrician knows in advance whether you want to breast feed.

Hemorrhoids. Another source of considerable annoyance is hemorrhoids. As stated in Chapter 3, hemorrhoids are extremely common in pregnant women. The rectal pressure during labor and the constipation following delivery act to promote swelling of the hemorrhoids in the first postpartum week. Salves and suppositories may relieve the pain; ice packs may decrease the swelling; the most effective therapy is prompt resumption of normal bowel function.

The Bowels. Routinely at many hospitals a laxative is given on the second night after delivery and, if necessary, an enema on the following day. It is rare for bowel function to become reestablished spontaneously before this time. If the discomfort caused by hemorrhoids and/or the episiotomy continues to interfere with the process of elimination, nightly laxatives or stool-softeners may be prescribed for a short while.

The Bladder. The baby presses on the bladder as it descends through the birth canal, and it may take several hours or even days before the elementary process of urination is completely normal. You will be encouraged to try to void within six or eight hours after delivery and if you cannot you may have to be catheterized. Catheterization involves the passage of a narrow plastic tube into your bladder. Although not the most pleasant experience in the world, it is not really painful. This initial inability to void, when it occurs, usually resolves itself promptly. A second type of bladder dysfunction which occasionally occurs is the inability to empty the bladder completely. This is also a transient affliction which requires catheterization for its relief.

The Blues. It is not uncommon or unnatural for a woman who has been keyed up for nine months over the prospect of having a baby to feel a little let down some time after the long-awaited event takes place. This sequence of events accounts for what is often referred to as "the baby blues." On or about the third day it is not unusual for a new mother to find herself uncontrollably weeping or unaccountably despondent over her new-found joy. There is no need for a psychiatrist here; this form of heartache is soon self-dispelled. If it persists after you go home, however, you'd better consult your obstetrician.

The Lochia. After delivery of the placenta there remains a fair amount of tissue lining the inside of the uterus, which has to be expelled in the same manner as the endometrium is shed during a menstrual period. Mixed with a little blood, this tissue comprises the lochia, a reddish discharge which may persist for two or three weeks or even as many as six weeks. It should never exceed a menstrual flow in daily volume and quite often it tapers off to mere staining after the first week. If it becomes profuse, your doctor will want to know about it. Needless to say you should wear an exterior type of pad rather than any sort of vaginal tampon at this time.

SERIOUS COMPLICATIONS

If any serious complications are to follow childbirth they will usually show up within the first week. Hemorrhage and infection are the most common types of trouble, and fortunately their incidence has been greatly reduced by modern techniques of delivery. The detection of your blood type, which was done on your initial visit to the doctor, was the first step to assure the ready availability of compatible blood for you in case of hemorrhage. Blood transfusions are simple, safe, and readily available in these days of the modern blood bank. And, of course, the infections, or "childbed fever," which used to claim the life of as many as one out of every four or five puerperal women before the days of Semmelweis and Pasteur, are now largely prevented by aseptic techniques and cured, when they do occur, by the fabulous antibiotic drugs. Other complications such as phlebitis and mastitis may develop, but they are rare and your doctor is trained to handle them. The average woman having a baby is young and healthy and need not fear complications.

ROOMING-IN

What It Means. "Rooming-in" means having the baby in the same room as the mother rather than in a nursery down the hall. It is an arrangement which has enjoyed increasing popularity in recent years. In most hospitals it is optional, in some it is mandatory, in a few it is forbidden. If it is optional at your hospital you will want to ponder the matter in advance. If you are anxious to have it, you should discuss its availability with the doctor at one of your first office visits. And, too, rooming-in means different things at different hospitals. The strictest rooming-in system involves having the baby with you twenty-four hours a day. Other hospitals offer a modified rooming-in plan whereby the baby is with you part of the day and in the nursery during the night and during nap periods. Rules vary, too, regarding the presence of visitors while the baby is with you. Usually at least the father is given this permission, enabling him to hold the baby and get acquainted. Sometimes children are allowed to visit in your room, sometimes in a separate visiting room, sometimes not at all.

Pros and Cons. There are several pros and cons to rooming-in. The primary issues are whether or not this is your first baby and how well you feel after the delivery. Since rooming-in implies not only the physical presence of the baby but also the necessity for the mother to minister unto her various needs, this experience is more valuable to the mothers of firstborns, for it gives them the opportunity to become acquainted with their babies and to learn how to handle them under supervision before taking them home. Taking home a first baby after having seen her only at feeding time in the hospital is often quite a jolt to the mother, one which can be largely circumvented by rooming-in.

But, on the other hand, the new mother needs rest in the hospital and she is going to get far less if the baby is constantly with her. Herein lie the advantages of the so-called modified rooming-in plan mentioned above, and often it is wise to defer rooming-in altogether for the first day or two until you are feeling rested and comfortable. Your doctor will help you work out a suitable plan. The situation is a little different for the woman who has children at home, who knows how to change a diaper, and who is to some degree exhausted by the combination of pregnancy and motherhood. She may prefer to enjoy the uninterrupted rest and solitude which she so richly deserves.

BREAST FEEDING

Breast or Bottle? "Which is better, breast feeding or bottle feeding?" Of course breast feeding is better. Have the American woman's breasts become so symbolic of sensuality that their function has actually been forgotten? Not quite, but evidently almost. All womankind used to breast-feed its babies; most European, Asian, African, and South American women still nurse their babies—yet only one third of the mothers in the United States fulfill this normal physiological function. Why? Largely because of a sort of misconceived national attitude toward breast feeding. If an American mother were seen nursing her baby in a public place, or even in her own living room, this would be regarded by many as mildly shocking, if not vulgar. Not

THE NURSING MOTHER.

so elsewhere. Surely, in the eyes of any truly discerning person, not to mention classic artists through the ages, a mother nursing her infant is one of the most tenderly beautiful sights one can behold.

Vanity probably prevents many a woman from nursing because of the notion that her breasts will droop more if she nurses than if she doesn't. There is absolutely no basis for this. If there is a tendency in this direction, it is more apt to be furthered by the more marked breast engorgement seen in nonnursing mothers.

Yet another reason more women don't breast-feed is the prevalent fear that there will be insufficient milk for the baby. This is obviously nonsense. If it were true, why didn't babies starve to death before bottles were invented?

Nor is there any correlation between the size of a woman's breasts and the abundance of her milk supply. Chinese women, whose breasts are quite small by American standards, are among the best nursers in the world.

Many women claim to prefer artificial feeding because their husbands can get up at night with the baby. It hardly seems necessary to point out that the fathers of breast-fed babies will be called upon to tend to many other nocturnal needs of their children over the years, whereas nighttime feedings usually last for only six to eight weeks.

And finally, there is the career woman who is anxious to return to her job. It is possible to work all day and continue nursing, but not until after six or eight weeks, when the milk supply has become firmly established.

Advantages of Breast Feeding. Why is nursing preferable to bottle feeding? One might simplify the answer to this by stating that woman's milk is, after all, meant for babies and cow's milk for calves, but this answer would be both oversimplified and incomplete. Since the composition of cow's milk is indeed quite different from that of human milk (chiefly in a greater amount of protein and a smaller amount of glucose or sugar), it is necessary to modify cow's milk in order to feed it to a baby. But even with present-day methods of doing this it is impossible to render cow's milk as ideal for babies as human milk. To illustrate this by just one difference, the protein of human milk is mostly lactalbumin, whereas that of cow's milk is mostly casein, the former being easier for a newborn baby to digest. There are also differences in the mineral and vitamin contents and obviously these differences exist because, let me repeat, one type of milk is best for human babies and the other is best for bovine babies.

As noted above, the nursing process hastens involution of the uterus, i.e., its return to normal size. True, the same effect can be wrought by drugs, but this is Nature's way of doing it.

The mother's antibodies to disease—the substances which render her resistant to colds and measles and poliomyelitis—are also secreted in her milk; in this way breast feeding helps protect the infant from sickness. Studies have conclusively shown that breast-fed babies are healthier.

If you have ever seen a friend preparing the formula for her bottle-fed baby you can certainly guess another of the many advantages of nursing: expediency. There is no pouring, no measuring, and no sterilizing.

The very fact that breast milk obviously doesn't have to be sterilized should suggest to you that still another advantage is that breast milk is sterile and hence safer for your baby. And, of course, breast milk is cheaper than store-bought facsimiles.

I have listed most of the commonly accepted physical advantages to breast feeding. In doing so I have purposefully left till last what is indisputably the greatest single argument for nursing, and that is the emotional factor. The act of nursing brings the mother closer to her child and the child closer to her mother. The instinct to suck is practically the only instinct with which we are born; this instinct is best satisfied by breast feeding. The nursing experience is also pleasurable for the mother. But far more important than these transient physical pleasures which each derives is the indefinable sense of love and security which they share, the one from giving, the other from receiving. Why is the painting of such a scene so beatific? Because it radiates love.

I have stressed the advantages of breast feeding with the vehemence which I think they deserve, but obviously there is another side to the story. Bottle-fed babies do survive. To me and to most other thinking obstetricians, however, it just stands to reason that breast feeding is the preferable way to feed a baby.

There are, of course, a few women who cannot or should not nurse—patients with active tuberculosis or diabetes, for example. And once in a long while there is a patient with such markedly inverted nipples that she cannot nurse. If the patient is not acutely ill and the nipples are at all normal, there is no physical reason why she cannot nurse.

Failure at Nursing. Why, then, are there women who try to nurse and fail? We have already established the fact that virtually every woman is physically able to nurse successfully. If, therefore, you have inferred that the explanation for most nursing failures is emotional, you couldn't be more right. There are few such vivid examples of the relationship of mind over matter as the phenomenon of nursing. If a new mother is afraid of her new responsibilities, if she is unduly worried about her health, her marriage, or even (and especially) her milk supply, or if she is even subconsciously leery of this nursing business, her chance of nursing successfully will be reduced. It's just as simple as that.

Success in nursing is mainly dependent upon and proportional to that vague but undeniable entity known as maternal drive. If you are determined to nurse and your baby is the most important thing in the world to you, you will succeed. If you are ambivalent about nursing, if you are more interested in returning to your job, or if the responsibilities of motherhood seem to overwhelm you, you are more likely to fail. In primitive societies all of the women belong to the first category and they all nurse; they are largely unaware that there is an alternative way of feeding a baby. In the stepped-up tempo of our ultracivilized society—our world of gadgets, psychoanalysts, synthetics, and tranquilizers—all too regrettably many of our young mothers fit into category number two.

Although one might bemoan the modern-day circumstances that mitigate against nursing, one cannot criticize the individual who does not nurse, for the simple reason that it isn't her fault. Sometime early in your pregnancy, you should discuss the possibility of nursing with your obstetrician. If you want to nurse and he believes that you can, then give it a try. There is no harm in trying and you will probably be surprised how easy and natural it is.

The Inconvenience of Nursing. Breast feeding is confining. It is inadvisable, as a general rule, to give a breast-fed baby more than an occasional bottle, for if you do so the baby will come to prefer the bottle, which provides sweeter milk at a faster rate. So you will be pretty much tied down to a three- or four-hour schedule for however long you nurse. This makes nursing inconvenient for the mother of other children and difficult for the mother who works. Obviously a mother can nurse and raise other children at the same time; it just requires a little reshuffling of her daily routine.

Regulation of Milk Supply. If nursing were difficult there would be far fewer people in the world today. It is an instinctive, natural act which requires little intelligence on the part of either mother or infant. Two basic facts with which you should be acquainted are (1) that the act of sucking is important in stimulating the milk to come in, and (2) that the amount of available milk is automatically regulated by the baby's needs.

You may nurse the first time in the delivery room, twelve hours later, or at some time in between. In any case, the baby will get no real milk for her efforts during the first few days. It is this early sucking, however, which initiates the onset of lactation on about the third or fourth day.

As for the supply being regulated by the demand, it is important for you to realize that the strongest impetus for milk to reenter the breasts is complete emptying of the breasts. A big hungry baby, for example, who needs, say, six ounces of milk every four hours, will empty the breast completely every time, and this will promote the relatively large supply which this baby needs. But the tiny baby who needs only an ounce or two per feeding will not empty the breasts completely at first, so the production of milk will be slowed down. Nature has a wonderful way of dealing with all these little problems.

Technique of Nursing. So what do you do the first time the baby is presented to you for nursing? No special preparation is necessary. When you put the nipple into the

baby's mouth (on top of her tongue) she may begin sucking right away. If she doesn't seem to understand what is
expected of her, stroke her cheek with your finger or with
the breast itself and this will usually cause the baby to
open her mouth and turn her head in the direction of the
cheek which has been stroked. For the first few days the
baby will probably not show much enthusiasm for two
reasons, first because she is not hungry and second because
you won't have much milk at this stage. If she tends to fall
asleep you should try to waken her by tickling her feet or
pretending to withdraw the nipple from her mouth for, as
mentioned above, it is important for her to suck in order
for your milk to come in. If you have any difficulty whatsoever (and most women do) with these initial attempts at
nursing, for heaven's sake don't feel embarrassed to ask for
help. The nursery nurses are experts in this business. And
don't be surprised if nursing hurts a bit at first, until your
nipples get toughened up.

After each nursing period is finished, prop the baby over
your left shoulder or sit her in your lap and gently pat her
back with your right hand. This ritual of "burping the
baby" will bring up the air which is unavoidably swallowed
while nursing, and which otherwise might cause the baby
to vomit. Even so, there will be occasional regurgitations
until the baby masters the business of swallowing. Even
though this regurgitation may sometimes look formidably
large, it will rarely represent an entire feeding, so don't feel
that it needs to be replaced by bottle.

Frequency of Feedings. During the first few days the
breast produces a rather thin yellow substance called colostrum. This is good for the baby too, for it contains the
mother's antibodies to disease. If your baby is kept in a
nursery down the hall she will be brought to you every four
hours, day and night, for feeding. The night feedings are
important, even in the hospital, in promoting lactation.
With rooming-in you can nurse your baby whenever you
feel she is hungry—at intervals of from two to four hours.
If the baby seems to be satisfied after sucking at one

breast, save the other one until the next feeding. If she doesn't seem satisfied after fifteen minutes on one side, offer her the other breast until she seems sated. Total nursing time should be limited to 20 minutes per feeding during the first week. The baby will empty the breast of 90 percent of its milk in the first ten minutes of conscientious sucking; additional time supplies more pleasure than nourishment. Excessive sucking will tend to make the nipples sore, especially in fair-skinned women. A variety of ointments can be used to protect tender nipples, but once they become injured by the baby to the point of being cracked, the entire success of the nursing program becomes endangered. It is therefore important that any tenderness or bleeding from the breasts be reported to the doctor immediately.

The obstetrician, the pediatrician, and the nursery nurses will help a new mother in her efforts to establish a satisfactory nursing regimen, but in the end the schedule and the technique must be worked out on an individual basis between each mother and her baby. Bear in mind this delicate balance: More frequent or prolonged nursing with both breasts will on the one hand tend to increase the milk supply and on the other hand tend to increase the danger of nipple trouble.

At home, after your milk supply has been established, you will be tempted to decide, irrevocably, between a rigid nursing schedule and feeding on demand. Please don't yield to this temptation. Either extreme will drive you, your husband, and your baby crazy. Each system has its merits, but a combination of them works best. What you want to achieve is a happy, well-nourished baby and peaceful, reasonably rested parents. Most babies of eight or more pounds do fine on feedings about four hours apart. If your baby cries after only three or three and a half hours, though, feed her. If she cries after only two or two and a half hours, try to temporize by giving her a pacifier or a few ounces of water, or simply by picking her up. And if she is still asleep, in the daytime, four hours after a feed-

ing, wake her up and feed her, for you will want her to
stop that nighttime feeding first. In other words: respond
to her demands within reason, but try to guide her toward
a schedule of feedings roughly four hours apart. She may
start to sleep through the night after six to eight weeks. If
she is still up at 4 A.M. when she is three months old, offer
her a pat, a pacifier, or a lullaby. A final word: To varying
degrees your nursing is bound to elicit some jealousy on
the part of your other children, your husband, and even
your poodle.

All of the above suggestions are very rough and general.
Although suitable for most mothers, they may not be suitable for you. If you want to learn more about nursing, I
would recommend that you read *Please Breast-Feed Your
Baby,* by Alice Gerard (New American Library, 1971). Or
contact the local representative of La Leche League (see
the white pages of your phone book), an organization
dedicated to the promotion of breast feeding.

Mind over Matter. The principal fear of every nursing
mother is that she will not have enough milk. For this
reason it is customary in most hospitals not to tell the
mother whether her baby is gaining weight or losing until
shortly before her discharge home. Every newborn baby
loses weight during the first few days anyway, no matter
how much she is fed, and the knowledge that her baby is
losing discourages most women. This discouragement in
turn acts to diminish the milk supply still further and a vi-
cious circle is started.

This control of the mind over the milk persists throughout the nursing process. If, for example, a woman nurses at
8 A.M. and then for some reason the baby cries for a few
hours and she becomes worried and agitated by this behavior, she will probably have less milk for the baby at noon;
if she then goes out to the movies and relaxes for a few
hours, she will probably have a super-abundance of milk
for the four o'clock feeding. Any sort of preoccupation on
the mother's part will momentarily lessen her supply of
milk. Conversely, the reflex between brain and breast even-

tually becomes so finely conditioned that milk literally spurts from the mother's nipple at the sound of her baby's cry.

How Long to Nurse. How long should you nurse? There is no universally right answer to this. Some aboriginal women nurse their babies for three or four years. Few American women want to continue after the seventh month, when the baby's first teeth appear. Actually any period in excess of three months is ample and laudable. Even a month is worthwhile. One or two weeks is perhaps better than not at all, though it would hardly be sensible to start to nurse with the intention of stopping so soon.

Breast Support. The need for wearing a bra during the nursing period depends on the size of the breasts. Generally, if the breasts are small a bra is unnecessary. But if the breasts are large or pendulous a good nursing brassiere is in order—night and day if it is more comfortable. These appliances are equipped with a variety of snaps and flaps that permit ready access for the baby without removal of the bra. Buy the kind you can unflap with one hand, while you are holding the baby with the other.

Cracked Nipples. The not infrequent combination of tender nipples and vigorous sucking may result in the formation of cracks (fissures) in the nipples, which will interfere with the nursing process. If allowed to progress unattended, this may lead to bleeding from the nipple or actual infection of the breast. As usual, the best treatment is preventative. The nipples must be kept scrupulously clean, a piece of dry gauze may be worn between them and the brassiere between feedings, and any dried milk should be removed from the area before nursing. If the nipples seem at all tender, report this to the nurse, who will provide you with an ointment to help toughen them. Simple exposure to the air may help.

If it actually becomes painful to nurse, a breast shield may be used. A breast shield consists of a conical piece of clear plastic with a rubber nipple attached to its apex. The plastic fits snugly around the nipple, the baby obtains milk by sucking the rubber nipple, and the mother's breast is thereby protected. Usually after using this device for a day or two the mother can resume nursing without further difficulty.

Maternal Infection. If the mother develops any form of infection it may become necessary to suspend nursing for fear of transmitting the infection to the baby. Meanwhile the breasts may be emptied every four hours either by manual expression, by hand pump, or by electric pump, thereby perpetuating the flow of milk. If the infection continues for more than a few days or is accompanied by a high fever, the milk supply may be curtailed to such an extent that later attempts at nursing will be defeated.

If you have to stop nursing suddenly, there is no medicine that will stop the production of milk. Just wear a good bra and, if your breasts are uncomfortable, apply an ice pack and take some Tylenol. The discomfort will subside in a day or two.

BOTTLE FEEDING

Advantages. Just as there are advantages to breast feeding, there are, of course, advantages to bottle feeding. The main physical advantage is that anyone can hold a bottle. The father, the nurse, the grandmother, and the baby-sitter can all share in the chore, if it is considered a chore, or they can help out if the mother must return to a job. To this extent artificial feeding is less confining, though it might be said in rebuttal that motherhood itself is confining and it is the mother who does most of the feeding anyway, regardless of the method. True, your husband can give the baby a bottle at night, if you can get him out of bed.

Modern-day formulas are scientifically designed to simulate the nutritional values of breast milk. Millions of strong, healthy babies are raised every year on formulas prepared by the manufacturer or mixed at home from combinations of canned milk, sugar, and water. And the warmth and love which a baby craves in association with her feeding can be supplied while holding a bottle too.

Preparation. If you are going to bottle-feed your baby, you will have to make a number of decisions before your baby is born. With regard to equipment, you will have to choose the type of nipple (*conventional shape* or Nuk, *pin holes* or cross-cut, *rubber* or silicone, *separate* or supplied with the bottle); the type of bottle (reusable glass, Pyrex, or plastic bottles; disposable plastic bottles; or *reusable holders with disposable liners*); and the type of formula (homemade from evaporated milk, corn syrup, and water; ready-to-serve liquid; *liquid concentrate*; or powder). Your pediatrician and your friends will help you make these decisions. I have italicized the most popular choices. Needless to say, the prices vary widely and, generally speaking, the more convenient the method the more expensive it will be. There is no medical advantage of one over the others.

Unless you use the ready-to-serve formula in disposable bottles with disposable nipples (the most expensive method, of course, but worth considering for an occasional trip), you will have to do some daily sterilizing of the bottles, nipples, and/or formula. For sterilizing bottles you will need about nine eight-ounce bottles, a large (eight- or nine-inch) pot with a lid, a bottle brush, and plastic or rubber-coated tongs. For storing nipples you will need an old peanut butter jar with its cap. And for making formula, a one-quart measuring cup and a funnel.

After homemade formula has been prepared or a can of commercially made formula has been opened, it must be refrigerated. Your mother would then warm it before offering it to you; you may serve it cold or at room temperature, just so long as you are consistent.

What you have just read will acquaint you, in a general way, with the options open to you. For more specific information you should consult your pediatrician and read one of the many baby-care books, such as Dr. Benjamin Spock's magnificent *Baby and Child Care* (Pocket Books, 1980).

Technique. The administration of a bottle to a baby does not require much in the way of tutelage, but in case the experience is new to you, here are a few pointers. Each feeding should take about twenty minutes. The trick to arriving at this approximate interval is to adjust the tightness of the bottle cap and the size of the hole in the nipple to the sucking power of your baby. Don't expect her to take the same amount of formula with each feeding; the quantity will vary with the time of day and her mood of the moment. Don't force her to take that last ounce; she may not want it. Unless you are using a collapsible liner, be sure to hold the bottle vertically enough so that the nipple is full of milk, not air, and remember to burp her once or twice per feeding. Above all, cuddle her while she's being fed; don't prop the bottle. The advice given about breast feeding by schedule or on demand (see pages 141–42) is equally applicable to bottle feeding.

THE NEWBORN BABY

Helplessness. No matter how many nieces and nephews they might have, most women are surprised by the diminutiveness and helplessness of their firstborn children. Newborn babies can't see, they can't make coordinated movements, they can't roll over, and they can't even raise their heads. They are only a little less dependent upon their mothers than they were before they were born. Among the few differences between intrauterine life and the first few weeks outside are that they will suck by instinct, they will breathe through reflex, they will urinate and defecate without volition, and they will feel pain. Satisfying their other needs is up to you.

Weight and Length. The weight of babies born at term ranges upward from 2,500 grams (5½ pounds). The average weight is about 3,400 grams (7 pounds 6 ounces), the average length 50 centimeters (20 inches). If a baby weighs less than 2,500 grams she is categorized as a premature infant.

Initial Appearance. The newborn may also look less beautiful in the flesh than she did in your dreams. As I said earlier, her head may appear misshapen because of its attempt to mold to the size of your pelvis. Various parts of her anatomy, especially the head and the feet, may be asymmetrical because of the particular positions they assumed in the uterus. There may be reddened areas on the baby's cheeks due to the forceps. The hands and feet may be quite blue. And whichever part of her delivered first may be swollen, due to the pressure upon it during labor. All of these physical alterations are transitory; most of them disappear spontaneously within two or three days.

The eyes of a newborn baby are closed most of the time, and they are apt to be a little reddened or swollen by the medicine which is dropped onto them in the delivery room. This medicine is used to prevent eye infections due to bacteria in the birth canal.

The umbilical cord is usually clamped or tied about half an inch from the skin of the abdomen. It dries up and falls off all by itself within four to ten days.

The breasts of a newborn, male or female, may be a little swollen (for as long as a month) and there may be actual lactation due to diffusion from the mother's bloodstream into the baby's, during the last days of pregnancy, of the hormones which produce lactation in the mother.

There are several soft spots in a baby's head. The one above the forehead is the largest and most easily felt. These little fontanels, as they are called, and the cracks which run between them enable the skull to increase in size as the baby grows. They do not close completely until about the eighteenth month.

During the early weeks of life the baby may unwittingly scratch her own face. The obvious solution to this is either to trim the baby's fingernails or to wrap them in the sleeves of her shirt.

A few days after birth the skin of the baby may become quite yellow. Unless there is Rh or blood-group trouble (see Chapter 5) this is usually the result of a normal physiological process which involves the destruction of the excess of red blood cells which most babies are born with. This type of jaundice should disappear within a few days. If it persists, call your pediatrician.

Weight Loss. Virtually all babies lose weight during the first few days. This loss is proportional to the weight of the infant; in the case of a seven-pound baby it is apt to be in the neighborhood of eight to ten ounces. The original birth weight is usually reached again by the end of the second week.

Circumcision. Circumcision of the newborn has been practiced by Jews, as a religious ritual, since Biblical times. This practice has been promoted as a health measure in this country since the turn of the century. Until recently over 90 percent of American males were circumcised. Since about 1970, however, the alleged benefits of this procedure have been largely debunked or disproved. According to the esteemed American Academy of Pediatrics, "there is no absolute medical indication for routine circumcision of the newborn." Nor, incidentally, is there any strong medical contraindication to the procedure. So the choice is yours, and it must be made on personal, emotional, or religious— not medical—grounds. If you decide in favor of the operation, you will be asked to sign a permit and it will be done by your obstetrician or pediatrician when your son is one to three days old. Ritual Jewish circumcisions are performed on the eighth day by a mohel.

The Premature. If your baby is born prematurely she may be placed in an incubator in a special nursery. Incubators provide more careful regulation of oxygen and humidity but—even more important—they also provide the scrupulous control of heat which these infants require. If your baby is premature she will probably have to remain in the hospital after you leave and until she weighs about 2,500 grams (5½ pounds).

Mistaken Identity. Cases of mistaken identity in the modern nursery are almost unheard of. Most babies are now braceleted at birth with plastic name tags and numbers which defy confusion. The baby's footprints are also taken in many hospitals. Ask for a copy to put in your baby book.

The Pediatrician. The pediatrician you chose during your pregnancy will see the baby in the hospital and give you an appointment for an office visit in about a month. You will want to establish an ongoing relationship with this specialist in child care, for he will play an important role in your family from now on.

HOSPITAL ROUTINES

The daily routine of a new mother follows a fairly standard pattern in most hospitals. You will probably be kept in bed for about twelve hours if you had regional anesthesia (epidural or spinal); otherwise you'll be up sooner. Limited activity is the rule. Although having a baby does not require any formal convalescence, you will notice a decided loss of stamina during the first weeks and you should take advantage of this brief opportunity to rest and be waited upon.

Visiting Hours. The visiting hours will vary from hospital to hospital and will depend somewhat upon whether or not you are rooming-in with your baby and whether you are in a private or semiprivate accommodation. At many hospitals the husband is allowed to visit any time of the day, even when the baby is in the room. The rules may be more stringent for other adult family members. Children are excluded by some hospitals because of the greater risk of their carrying an infection. Photography is usually permitted, but no flash bulbs.

Medical Routines. Your finger will probably be pricked in order to determine what effect, if any, the delivery had upon your blood count. An enema may be given in order to get the bowels working again. An analgesic drug such as codeine or Tylenol will be available if you are uncomfortable, but you will probably have to ask for it every time you want it. There is no harm in taking it, however, and no need for you to be in pain, so ask for it as often as you like. It is difficult to sleep in the hospital for many reasons, such as activities in the corridor and cries from the nursery. So don't be afraid to take a sleeping pill at night; you won't become addicted and it is important for you to get your sleep. Naps are encouraged in the daytime too; take advantage of the opportunity. The nurse will show you how to take care of your perineum, for it is important that it be kept as clean and dry as possible. Sanitary napkins and belts are usually supplied by the hospital. A heat lamp may be used once or twice a day, too, in order to promote healing of the episiotomy.

The Birth Certificate. The birth registrar will want to know the name you have chosen for the baby within forty-eight hours. It is surprising how difficult this decision often is. In case you have any trouble in this regard, let me give you two personal suggestions. Don't give the baby a family name. If this advice seems strange, let me assure you that it makes good psychiatric sense. Many are the victims of this practice who have unduly suffered from the inane subconscious lifelong struggle to emulate (or defy) their namesakes. And if you can't agree with your husband in the choice of a perfect name (as is usually the case), you can probably agree upon the plan that you name all the girls and he the boys, or vice versa.

Every birth in the United States is registered (by the obstetrician) with the state and federal Bureaus of Vital Statistics. Some states send "birth cards" or unofficial birth certificates to the baby's parents. In order to obtain definitive proof of the birth, however, you must apply for a certified copy of the birth certificate. This is done by writing to the Bureau of Vital Statistics of the state where the birth occurred, stating the baby's name, sex, date of birth, parents' names, and the purpose for which the copy is needed.* There is usually a fee of about $2.00 for this service.

PREPARATION FOR GOING HOME

You will want clothes for yourself and the baby when you leave the hospital. Few women are quite ready to wear their ordinary clothes so soon after delivery, so they must swallow their pride and wear a maternity outfit. As for the baby, this is an individual matter. A newborn baby's wardrobe may cost anywhere from $5.00 to $500, and I've seen a few that must have cost even more. Unless you have a staff of servants to take care of it, it is usually best to buy only the most rudimentary sort of layette. The grandparents and baby showers will provide most of the frills anyway and chances are they will rarely be worn.

The Layette. Under the age of six months a baby needs diapers, shirts, sheets, a blanket, and that's about all. Most mothers today elect to use disposable diapers, despite their adding to our pollution problem. They come in sizes for under and over twenty-three-pound infants. Adhesive tabs preclude the need for pins. A diaper service will deliver a weekly supply of cloth diapers. To save money, launder your own; buy two dozen to start with. If you use cloth diapers you will need rubber or plastic panties to go with them.

The simplest type of baby shirt is the classic buttonless model which ties with strings and has tabs which can be pinned to the diaper; six will do. Get half a dozen of the simplest possible flannel or stockinet nighties—preferably those which tie at the bottom—or pajamas with feet. Stay away from buttons and buy everything in size one. A knitted, hooded suit is ideal for winter outings, or a zippered blanket-bag (called "bunting") which covers the baby

---

* The exception to this rule: births in New York City, where application must be made to the Bureau of Vital Statistics of the borough in which the birth occurred.

from chin to toe. Cloth diapers or receiving blankets can be used to protect you from inevitable burps and poops. Baby wash cloths and towels also come in handy. Dresses, hats, booties, and the like are superfluous items, needed only for dress-up parties and family portraits.

The weight of the blankets will depend on the climate where you live. Home-knit ones are perfect. You will also need half a dozen mattress pads to put under the baby and a couple of waterproof sheets to cover the mattress.

The baby's bed is a matter of individual choice. If you still have your grandmother's cradle, fine. If you can borrow your neighbor's bassinet, better yet. Beware, however, of lead paint on hand-me-down furniture, for babies love to eat it. If you are going to have to buy something perhaps I can make a suggestion. To begin with, there are bassinets, cribs, youth beds, and adult beds. If you start with a bassinet you may find yourself buying all four—not a very economical approach. Since a baby is just as happy for at least three months in a wicker laundry basket, a dresser drawer, or any similar receptacle, a fancy bassinet is hardly essential. As a matter of fact she will be equally happy in a crib, which can be used for the first few years. She can then be graduated to an adult bed or studio couch, thereby shortening the list from four items to two.

Bathinets are also optional equipment. They provide a nice table-height place to bathe the baby and a nice level surface on which to dress her, but it is just as easy to give the bath in a big enamel or plastic tub or even a sink, with a towel on the bottom to prevent slipping. In the bath area prepare a table, tray, or shelf with the toilet articles you will need: swabs, absorbent cotton, corn starch (for rashes), and soap. When not in use, keep the points of the safety pins buried in a cake of soap. Don't forget a diaper pail for under the sink.

Some people seem to feel that a baby carriage is as important as a high chair. Perhaps it is if you live in an apartment. Otherwise it is an anachronism. More suited to our times are the body carriers (for toting a baby on your chest, side, or back), the car seat (for strapping a baby in during a car ride), the collapsible carryall (for providing a bed away from home while visiting friends), and the inclined infant-seat (a portable throne from which she can watch you work). Select what you need most; you won't need them all.

Baby scales are unnecessary. Weighing a baby after every feeding or even as often as once a day will lead to constant confusion. Healthy babies don't have to be weighed at home; your pediatrician will take care of this. If you can't resist weighing her or if someone insists on buying scales for you, make sure they are balance scales, not spring scales, and don't use them more often than twice a week.

The Final Exam. Just before your discharge from the hospital your doctor may perform a final pelvic examination. Since this is apt to be a moderately uncomfortable procedure at this time, especially in the presence of a healing episiotomy, and since there is little to be gained from it, many doctors prefer to postpone this exam until the postpartum visit in the office. If you have any last-minute problems or questions, however, this is the time to ask them.

Length of Hospital Stay. Your grandmother, after giving birth, remained in the hospital for two or three weeks after delivery. She didn't even get out of bed the first week. It is now know that this protracted convalescence caused more harm than good. In the 1950s and 1960s the new mother stayed in the hospital for a week, but now the hospital room rates are so astronomical that most women go home in three to five days. If you choose to go home sooner than this you may have to leave your baby in the nursery.

9

Motherhood at Home

After nine months of planning and one week in the hospital, the moment for you to return home with your baby has finally arrived. It is a triumphant, exalting, memorable event. Don't mess it up.

THE FIRST DAY

The Return. Returning home is an event to be shared and cherished with your husband—no one else. If you happen to live in a three-room walk-up apartment and your parents or your in-laws beg you to bring the baby home to their twenty-room country estate, take the baby to your own three rooms. Learn to love her and live with her and raise her by yourself. If Grandma wants to come over to your place and help you cook or clean or do the laundry, fine; but you take charge of the baby.

The Siblings. If you have other children at home, your return should be planned in advance with their tender feelings in mind. They want to see you, not the baby. No matter how convincing they may be to the contrary, they are going to hate the baby—most especially on this crucial day. So shower them with attention and show them the baby later, with a minimum of fuss and a maximum of reassurance that you still love them too.

The Fatigue. The first day home will be emotionally and physically exhausting. It's best not to go home until midday. Don't tackle the housework yet. Don't invite your friends over yet. Enjoy your family and get to bed early.

HELP

The Family. Lots of women manage beautifully during the first few weeks at home with no help other than the little they receive from their husbands. Some self-sacrificing new fathers plan their vacations to coincide with the due date for this reason. In many other cases one of the new grandmothers lends a helping hand. Any hand is helpful during the first few weeks, especially if the hand is properly used.

HELP AT HOME. Let *her* wash the dishes; *you* wash the baby.

Nurse or Maid? If none of these alternative sources of assistance is available to you, you may be in the market for a baby nurse. It has become very fashionable to hire these professional nannies to take over the early baby care. You can usually find one through a friend or through an agency. Sometimes you'll get a registered nurse, more often a practical nurse, and most often a specialized baby-sitter.

What happens when you hire a baby nurse? Most likely you will find that she takes over the baby while you take over the housework. Fewer and fewer baby nurses these days deign to wash a dish or mop a floor. The disadvantages of such a setup are apparent. If this is the only kind of baby nurse you can get, you will be better off with a part-time maid. The baby is yours. Take care of her yourself.

ACTIVITIES

Taboos. The advice given to puerperal patients varies from doctor to doctor, but in general it will include abstinence from tub baths, douches, and sexual intercourse. You may be asked to refrain from baths for two weeks, douches for four, and sex for six. I find, since there is difference of opinion on this subject, that it is simpler for the patient to avoid all three of these activities until her first postpartum visit in six weeks. Wear a pad, not a tampon, for the first two weeks.

Daily Doings. Showers and shampoos are permissible. Lifting and climbing should be limited as much as is feasible. As for the everyday activities of housework, driving, shopping, and socializing, it seems ridiculous to me to lay down any specific rules. Most new mothers can feel their own way in this regard; I find that they vary tremendously in their desires and abilities to recuperate. The same instructions, for example, could hardly be given to women with four other children and no help and to women with a maid and no other children.

Obviously you will not want to go out the day you get home and play three sets of tennis or move the furniture. If you overdo, you will tire. Nature will help you set the proper pace. Take a nap every day, if you possibly can, especially while the baby is getting you up at night. By and large it is preferable to devote most of your first week to care of the baby. This will keep you plenty busy. Your mother, nurse, maid, friends, or—if worse comes to worst—your husband can help with the housework. The second week you will probably begin to feel cooped up. If so, there is no reason why you can't go out for a short while. By the third or fourth week you should feel as good as new.

Calisthenics. Flabbiness of the abdominal wall is a universal complaint which becomes louder after each successive pregnancy. The modern woman wants to know what can be done about it. Any form of abdominal exercise will help to remedy the situation and every new mother is inevitably involved in plenty of bending and stooping in connection with her daily chores. But if you want to feel that you are making a more definite effort in this direction, any calisthenic which tightens the abdominal muscles will fill the bill. Lie flat on your back and lift your legs stiffly, one at a time, and then together. Or, if you really want to suffer, lie on your back, and with your knees unbent lift your heels about one inch off the floor; then inscribe tiny circles in the air with your toes without letting your feet touch the ground.

DIET

After delivery the mother can usually resume her normal eating habits. If you haven't lost as much weight as you had hoped, however, you will want to reduce your calories accordingly. You will know now the importance of beginning your next pregnancy at your ideal weight. Nursing mothers require the same scrupulous dietary regulation as they did before delivery. They should continue to eat well-balanced meals, with emphasis on protein, iron, calcium, and vitamins. Continue to take your prenatal capsules, with fluoride, as long as you're nursing, and try to consume a quart and a half of milk or its equivalent every day. No food you eat while nursing will adversely affect the baby, but you should check with your doctor before taking any drugs.

MENSTRUATION

Most nonnursing mothers have their first menstrual period within eight weeks. It may appear any time after the first month, and this first period is apt to be peculiar. It may be profuse or prolonged, scanty, or intermittent.

Nursing mothers, on the other hand, may not have any periods at all as long as they continue to nurse. There are many exceptions, though; it is not unusual for the first period to occur about four months after delivery. It has long been thought that it is impossible to become pregnant again while nursing. Lactation does, indeed, provide protection against pregnancy which is fairly reliable, but not completely so. In other words, don't count on it. It is also widely believed that a pregnancy which develops during the nursing process will be adversely affected. Not so.

COMPLICATIONS

It is unusual for complications to arise more than a week after delivery. When unexpected symptoms do develop, however, it is good to know what they mean. First on the list of possibilities is bleeding. Delayed hemorrhage may occur any time during the first month. Occasionally it is due to retention in the uterus of a small fragment of placental tissue, which must then be removed by curettage. More often it is due simply to involution of the site of placental attachment and requires no specific treatment, except perhaps for Ergotrate, an oxytocic drug which your doctor will prescribe.

Infection is likewise rare after leaving the hospital. The most common sites of infection at this stage are the breasts, the urinary system, and the uterus. Fever is common with all three conditions. Breast infection (mastitis) will manifest itself through tenderness and reddening of the breast. Infection of the bladder (cystitis) or kidney (pyelitis) may be associated with frequency of urination and a burning sensation while voiding. Infections of the uterus (endometritis) will usually cause a foul-smelling vaginal discharge. Any such symptoms should, of course, be reported immediately to your doctor.

When you stop nursing, you may be troubled with some degree of breast engorgement. The breasts may become hard and painful. As mentioned in connection with non-nursing mothers, there is no specific treatment for this condition. The best remedies include good round-the-clock breast support, Tylenol, and ice bags. Limit unnecessary fluids but continue to drink as usual at mealtime. The swelling will subside in two or three days.

BABY CARE

As an obstetrician, I am not qualified to advise you upon the all-important subject of baby care. This is the pediatrician's role. As the father of four, however, perhaps I may be permitted a few paragraphs on the nonmedical aspects of this subject.

Taking home the first baby is a somewhat frightening experience. Such complete responsibility for a human life will seem a little overwhelming at first. But pregnancy and labor were strange new challenges only nine months ago and you have survived them, probably with greater equanimity than you expected. Baby care can hardly be any more difficult, in view of the millions of mothers who seem to have mastered it. Of course you want your child to surpass all others in the emotional, intellectual, and physical spheres. And you want to assure these assets to her from the very first month.

No matter what you desire for your child's future, right now it is vitally important that you understand the capabilities and the limitations of a newborn infant. As for her capabilities, they are pretty limited: she can suck, wiggle, cry, urinate, defecate, and that's all. Her powers of sight and cerebration are very, very limited. She can feel you, but she can't see you. She has lain curled up in your womb so long that she can hardly extend her arms and legs, and she can't coordinate her muscles enough to reach out for something she wants. Above all she will instinctively cry from pain or hunger, but she will not cry, at this age, because she is scheming for attention.

A newborn baby needs only four things: warmth, food, sleep, and love. The warmth is easy. Bundle her well in winter weather; a light blanket will do in a well-heated room; a shirt should suffice in the heat of summer. There is no reason the food should be a problem. She will cry when she's hungry. It will soon become apparent that she is hungry every four, or sometimes every three, hours. If she cries at shorter intervals, don't try to read any diabolical motive or frightful malady into her cry. No one can interpret a baby's every cry; don't try. It is to be expected that an infant will cry without reason for one or two hours a day.

This, the baby's crying, is the one aspect of early parenthood that drives most novices up the wall. Unfortunately, the written word is not very useful on this score, but I will give you this general advice: Don't pick up the baby every time she cries and don't ignore her every time. As with most such issues, a middle road is best. You will probably have to respond to cries in the night for about eight to twelve weeks. By then the baby will probably be able to sleep for six hours at a stretch. If she tries to turn day into night, don't let her—i.e., wake her, if necessary, for each daytime feeding.

As for love, you cannot give a newborn baby too much love. You can't spoil a baby this soon. The most propitious time to demonstrate your love is, of course, at feeding times. Whether you breast-feed your baby or bottle-feed her, cuddle her, kiss her, hug and caress her. Food is a baby's greatest physical need. Mealtimes are her most wakeful moments. Let her associate the fulfillment of this need and her earliest awareness of the world with love.

THE POSTPARTUM VISIT

Your doctor will probably want to see you in his office four to six weeks after the delivery. In many ways this may be regarded as the most important appointment since the very first one, about nine months ago. He will want to know all that has transpired in the past six weeks with regard to your breasts, your menstruation, your general health, and your baby. Your weight, breasts, abdomen, and genitalia will be rechecked to see what effect the pregnancy has had upon them.

The Pelvic Exam. Pelvic examination at this time is important. The opening of your vagina may be more relaxed because of the delivery or, if you had a proper episiotomy, it may actually be a little tighter than before. It is almost routine at this time to discover an erosion or "sore" on the cervix, indicating that this organ has not yet completely healed. Further healing may occur spontaneously, it may be hastened by warm vinegar douches, or it may eventually require treatment with cautery.

Another common and even less significant finding at this time is retroversion or tipping back of the uterus. This is a normal condition before pregnancy in many women. Fifty years ago retroversion was held by the medical profession to be responsible for all sorts of female troubles from backache to sterility. It is now known to be a harmless variation in anatomy which has no more medical significance than brown eyes. Some doctors prescribe the "knee-chest exercise" to help "correct" this condition. The patient is told to position herself in bed with her shoulders flat against the mattress, the knees flexed under her and spread about a foot apart, the buttocks up in the air. Assuming this position for twenty minutes twice a day will bring the uterus forward for forty minutes a day, but I doubt that it has any permanent anatomical effect and I doubt that such an effect would be worth striving for anyway.

Birth Control. Now is the time to discuss family planning with your obstetrician. There is no valid medical reason why a healthy woman cannot have her pregnancies one right after the other. Some women prefer it this way, so that their children will grow up together and the parents will finish with diapers once and for all. Others prefer to space their children two, three, or more years apart. If you decide on the latter course, you should be prepared to choose a birth-control method at this postpartum visit.

In order for you and your husband to reach a more intelligent decision on what type of birth control you want, I shall briefly describe the more popular methods. You will then, of course, want to discuss your preference with your obstetrician, for there may be medical reasons why a particular method may not be suitable for you.

The Pill. Taken as directed—for twenty, twenty-one, or twenty-eight days a month (depending on the type of pill) —oral contraception is 100 percent effective. It works by preventing ovulation. If you are nursing your baby you should use another form of birth control. The Pill is not for you if you have bad veins, migraine, fibroids, hypertension, diabetes, or liver disease. For healthy young women, however, the Pill is practically harmless.

The I.U.D. Made of plastic, sometimes wrapped with copper wire, and designed in a variety of modernistic shapes, the intrauterine device is inserted by the obstetrician and allowed to remain in place for several years if it does not cause trouble. Sometimes it causes the menstrual periods to be heavier; occasionally it falls out. For many women, though, it provides excellent protection without requiring interference with the sex act.

The Diaphragm. This is the method your mother probably used. The diaphragm is a thin sheet of rubber or latex stretched over a collapsible metal ring. It can be obtained, on prescription, after the doctor determines your size. Smeared with a spermatocidal cream or jelly, the diaphragm is inserted into the vagina before intercourse and removed six or more hours later. Although about as reliable as the I.U.D., its insertion can interfere with foreplay and many find it messy.

The Condom. The fourth and last of the reliable methods, the condom is the only one under the man's control. It is especially effective when used in conjunction with a spermatocidal jelly. Its chief disadvantage is a lessening of the perception of sexual sensation by both partners.

Jellies, Creams, Tablets, and Foams. Although easy to use and available without prescription, these methods are inferior to the four described above. If your sex life is sporadic, you need extra lubrication, and/or you don't demand nearly complete protection, try them. Otherwise, pick one of the four more reliable methods described above.

Rhythm. The only method approved by the Roman Catholic Church, rhythm entails abstaining from sex around the time of ovulation. With regular periods this means sleeping alone for seven to ten days a month— longer, of course, if your periods are unpredictable. Your doctor will help you work out a schedule. Practiced religiously by women with regular menstrual cycles, it does work.

Lactation. It is widely believed that it is impossible for a woman to get pregnant while she is nursing. This is not true. Nursing does have some contraceptive effect (through suppressing ovulation), but not nearly enough to rely on.

The End. After your final examination you will return to your obstetrician's office to hear whether you have completely mended, to ask whatever last-minute questions you have, and to revel in the satisfaction of what you've accomplished. If you are back to normal, you will be allowed to resume tub baths, intercourse, and all your usual activities. You can lead a normal life again—better, bigger, busier, and more rewarding. Take good care of that baby and come back next year for your checkup.

Glossary of Obstetrical Terms

The definitions in this glossary are limited to the meanings used in this book.

ABORTION: the termination of a pregnancy before the end of the twentieth week; spontaneous abortion and miscarriage are synonymous.

ABORTUS: the products of an abortion.

AFTERBIRTH: the placenta, fetal membranes, and umbilical cord, which are expelled from the uterus after the birth of the baby.

AFTERPAINS: the lower abdominal cramps sometimes felt for a few days after delivery, caused by contractions of the uterus.

AMBULATION: walking; getting out of bed.

AMNIOCENTESIS: the insertion of a needle into the uterine cavity in order to remove some of the amnoitic fluid.

AMNIOTIC: pertaining to the amnion, one of the fetal membranes (e.g., the amniotic sac and the amniotic fluid).

ANALGESIA: loss of pain perception.

ANALGESIC: a drug such as aspirin, codeine, Tylenol, and Demerol, which produces analgesia.

ANESTHESIA: loss of sensation produced by various drugs, gases, and vapors. General anesthesia involves the entire body (e.g., ether, gas). Regional anesthesia involves a limited area of the body. The types of regional anesthesia used in obstetrics to numb the birth canal include spinal (or saddle block), whereby a drug is introduced into the spinal canal; epidural, whereby a drug is introduced into the space outside the spinal canal, where the spinal nerve roots emerge; caudal, a type of epidural whereby a drug is introduced through the base of the spine; and local (or pudendal), whereby a drug is injected near the nerve endings which supply the vagina and perineum.

ANESTHESIOLOGIST: a physician who specializes in administering anesthesia (as opposed to an anesthetist, who need not be a physician).

ANGIOMA: literally, a tumor of blood vessels; the so-called spider angiomas of pregnancy are formed by tiny blood vessels in the skin, arranged in the form of a spider.

ANOMALY: deviation from the norm; deformity.

ANTEPARTUM: before labor or delivery; prenatal.

ANTIBODY: a substance in the blood which reacts specifically against foreign bodies such as the Rh antigen.

ANTIGEN: a substance which, when introduced into the blood-stream of an individual who does not normally possess this substance, causes the production of antibodies.

ASEPSIS: the absence of bacteria or germs.

AUSCULTATION: listening, usually with a stethoscope.

BARBITURATE: the general term for a variety of drugs which are derived from barbituric acid and used to produce sleep.

BETAMETHASONE: a cortisonelike steroid which helps to prevent respiratory distress in premature infants when given to the mother twenty-four hours before delivery.

BREECH: the buttocks.

CATGUT: a type of thread used as a suture material in surgical procedures, manufactured from the intestinal lining of sheep.

CATHETER: a tubular instrument made of rubber, metal, plastic, or glass and used to drain urine from the bladder.

CATHETERIZATION: the procedure whereby urine is drawn from the bladder by the introduction of a tube (catheter).

CAUTERY: the searing of tissues by heat.

CEPHALOPELVIC DISPROPORTION: the situation which pertains when the fetal head is large in proportion to the size of the maternal pelvis.

CERVICAL: pertaining to the cervix.

CERVIX: the "neck" of the womb; that part of the womb which protrudes into the vagina.

CHROMOSOME: the small bodies, present in the nucleus of every cell, which contain the genes.

CILIA: the hairlike processes which line certain body organs such as the fallopian tubes.

COITUS: sexual intercourse.

COLOSTRUM: the thin yellow fluid secreted by the breasts during the first few days after delivery (and sometimes during pregnancy), differing from true breast milk in containing more protein, vitamins, and minerals.

CONCEPTION: pregnancy or the act of becoming pregnant.

CONCEPTUS: the products of conception; the fetus and placenta.

CONTRACEPTION: birth control; the prevention of pregnancy.

CURETTAGE: scraping the uterine cavity with an instrument (a curette) introduced through the cervical canal; a minor operation done in obstetrics in order to cause an abortion, to complete the process of a miscarriage, or to evacuate placental fragments after delivery.

CYSTITIS: infection of the bladder.

DEFECATION: the act of moving the bowels.

DEMEROL: a synthetic drug to relieve pain (trade name).

DIURETIC: any drug whose action increases the production of urine and hence the elimination of body fluids.

DOPTONE: an ultrasonic device used to produce an audible rendition of the fetal heartbeat (trade name).

ECLAMPSIA: that form of toxemia of pregnancy which is characterized by all of the features of preeclampsia plus convulsions and/or coma.

ECTOPIC: out of place; an ectopic pregnancy is one which is located outside the uterine cavity, usually in the fallopian tube.

EDEMA: the accumulation of excessive amounts of fluid in the body tissues.

EMBRYO: the term used to designate the product of conception between the third and fifth weeks of pregnancy.

ENDOMETRITIS: infection of the endometrium.

ENDOMETRIUM: the glandular innermost lining of the uterus, which is shed during menstruation; during pregnancy it forms the bed for the ovum and at a later stage it becomes incorporated into the placenta.

ENGORGEMENT: congestion or filling; engorgement of the breasts is due to an increased flow of blood and lymph.

EPISIOTOMY: the incision in the perineum which is made just before delivery in order to prevent tears.

ERGOTRATE: a powerful oxytocic which is sometimes administered after delivery of the placenta (trade name).

EROSION: a sore, similar to an abrasion in appearance.

ERYTHROBLASTOSIS: the disease which may affect infants born of Rh-negative mothers and Rh-positive fathers.

ESTROGEN: the ovarian hormone which is secreted throughout the menstrual cycle and pregnancy and is essential to development of the endometrium and feminization of the body.

ETIOLOGY: cause.

FASCIA: connective tissue which protects, joins, or supports certain parts of the body.

FERTILIZATION: penetration of an ovum by a sperm.

FETAL: pertaining to the fetus.

FETUS: the term used to designate the product of conception between the fifth week and delivery.

FIBROIDS: benign uterine tumors composed of muscle and connective tissue.

FLATULENCE: the presence of excessive amounts of intestinal gas (flatus).

FONTANELS: the spaces formed at the junctions of the cranial bones in an infant.

FORCEPS: an instrument used to extract the baby's head from the birth canal.

FUNDUS: the upper muscular part of the uterus, which contracts in labor.

GENE: a factor, present in the chromosomes of every cell, which determines the hereditary characteristics of the individual.

GENITALIA: the genitals; the organs concerned in the process of reproduction.

GESTATION: pregnancy.

GRAVID: pregnant.

GYNECOLOGY: the branch of medicine which deals with diseases of the female organs.

HEARTBURN: a burning sensation in the mid-chest, associated with a spasm of the esophagus.

HEMOGLOBIN: the protein substance in red blood cells which contains iron and is responsible for the transportation of oxygen from the lungs to the body tissues.

HEMORRHAGE: the loss of more than a pint of blood.

HEMORRHOIDS: abnormally distended veins in the area of the anus, colloquially known as piles.

HORMONE: the internal secretion from a gland, such as insulin from the pancreas and estrogen from the ovary, or from other tissue, such as prostaglandin.

HYPERTENSION: high blood pressure; in pregnancy, blood pressure higher than 140/90.

HYSTEROTOMY: a miniature cesarean section, a method of performing an abortion.

INERTIA: "uterine inertia" is a term used to connote desultory or weak labor.

INTRAUTERINE: within the uterus.

INVOLUTION: the return of the postpartum uterus to normal size.

I.U.D.: an intrauterine contraceptive device.

JAUNDICE: a yellow discoloration of the skin, nail beds, and eyeballs, due to the deposition in the tissues of bile pigments or, as in the case of the newborn infant, of the breakdown products of red blood cells.

LACTATION: the secretion of milk by the breasts.

LAPAROSCOPE: a hollow metal tube which can be inserted through the abdominal or vaginal wall in order to visualize the abdominal organs and, if sterilization is being done, to sear the fallopian tubes with cautery.

LEUKEMIA: a malignant disease of the white blood cells.

LEUKORRHEA: abnormal vaginal discharge.

LIGHTENING: the descent of the fetus's head into the maternal pelvis, which may occur during the last few weeks of pregnancy.

LOCHIA: the discharge of blood, mucus, and endometrial tissue which is seen during the first one to six weeks following childbirth.

LYMPH: a body fluid resembling blood plasma and containing white blood cells.

LYMPHATIC: pertaining to lymph.

MASTITIS: inflammation of the breast.

MEMBRANES: paper-thin sheets of tissue; the fetal membranes consist of two layers, the amnion and the chorion, which become fused in the form of a sac, which contains the fetus and the amniotic fluid.

MENSTRUATION: the monthly discharge of blood and endometrium from the uterus; menstrual period.

MOLDING: the process by which the fetal head changes in shape as it is squeezed through the birth canal.

MORPHINE: a powerful pain reliever derived from the poppy flower, administered intramuscularly.

MUCOUS PLUG: the clear, sticky secretion which fills the cervical canal and is expelled at the onset of labor.

MULTIPARA: a woman who has given birth to more than one baby.

NARCOSIS: the stuporous state produced by narcotic drugs.

NARCOTIC: a drug which is capable of relieving pain and producing sleep.

NULLIPARA: a woman who has not given birth to a baby.

OVULATION: the extrusion of an ovum from the ovary.

OVUM: the egg or female germ cell.

OXYTOCIC: a drug which causes the pregnant or puerperal uterus to contract.

PAP SMEAR: a test discovered by Dr. George Papanicolaou for detecting cancer of the cervix by microscopic examination of cells in the vagina.

PAROUS: having given birth to one or more babies.

PARTURIENT: related to childbirth; the woman in labor.

PARTURITION: the act of childbirth.

PATHOLOGICAL: abnormal, diseased.

PEDIATRICIAN: a doctor who specializes in the care of children.

PELVIMETRY: measurement of size and shape of the bony pelvis; this may be done by pelvic exam or by X-ray.

PENTOTHAL: a short-acting barbiturate administered intravenously to induce anesthesia (trade name).

PERINEUM: that area of female anatomy between the vagina and the rectum.

PERISTALSIS: the wavelike contractions of tubular organs which enable their contents to be propelled forward.

PHLEBITIS: inflammation of a vein.

PHYSIOLOGICAL: normal, as opposed to pathological.

PITOCIN: an oxytocic which is secreted by the pituitary gland to stimulate labor naturally; it is also prepared commercially as a drug to stimulate labor artificially; sometimes referred to colloquially as "Pit" (trade name).

PLACENTA: afterbirth; the organ, attached to the uterus, through which the fetus acquires oxygen and nourishment and excretes its waste products.

PLACENTA PREVIA: the condition in which the placenta is attached to the lowermost part of the uterus, thereby encroaching upon the cervical opening.

POSTPARTUM: following childbirth.

PREECLAMPSIA: that form of toxemia of pregnancy characterized by edema, hypertension, and/or albuminuria.

PREMATURE INFANT: an infant weighing less than 2,500 grams (5½ pounds) at birth.

PREMIE: a premature infant.

PRIMIPARA: a woman who has given birth to one baby.

PROGESTERONE: the ovarian hormone which is secreted after ovulation and is responsible for preparation of the endometrium for implantation of the fertilized egg.

PROGNOSIS: outlook; forecast.

PUERPERAL: pertaining to the puerperium.

PUERPERIUM: the first four weeks following childbirth.

PULMONARY: pertaining to the lungs.

PYELITIS: infection of the kidney.

QUICKENING: fetal movement.

RETROVERSION: tipping of the womb backward toward the rectum rather than forward toward the bladder.

RH FACTOR: a substance present in the red blood cells of rhesus monkeys and 85 percent of humans.

RHOGAM: a specially prepared gamma globulin containing Rh antibodies which prevent maternal sensitization to the Rh factor (trade name).

RUBELLA: German measles.

SHOW: the mixture of blood and mucus which is discharged from the vagina before and during labor.

SONOGRAM: see ultrasonogram.

SPERM: the male germ cell.

SPERMATOCIDAL: capable of killing sperm.

STAPHYLOCOCCUS: a common type of bacterium which may cause infections in various parts of the body, especially the skin.

STRIAE: the linear skin markings present on the abdomen and breasts during and after pregnancy, due to stretching.

SUTURE: the thread with which the surgeon sews.

TERM: in obstetrical parlance, a pregnancy is at term between the thirty-eighth and forty-second weeks, i.e., from two weeks before to two weeks after the due date.

TETRACYCLINE: one of the many types of antibiotic.

TOXEMIA: the diseases of pregnancy known as preeclampsia and eclampsia.

TRAUMA: injury.

TRIMESTER: a period of three months; the first, second, and third three-month stages of pregnancy are described as the first, second, and third trimesters.

TYLENOL: a synthetic drug to relieve pain (trade name).

ULTRASONOGRAM: (sonogram) a picture made with high-frequency sound waves, used to locate soft-tissue structures within the body.

UMBILICAL CORD: a cord about half an inch in diameter and about twenty inches long, containing fetal blood vessels and extending from the navel of the fetus to the interior surface of the placenta.

UTERINE: pertaining to the uterus.

UTERUS: the womb; a hollow muscular organ in the female pelvis, which acts as the source of menstruation and the site of gestation.

VARICOSE VEINS: abnormally swollen or dilated veins.

VARICOSITY: a varicose vein.

VASCULAR: supplied with blood vessels.

VAS DEFERENS: the tube which conducts sperm from the testicles.

VASECTOMY: an operation to sterilize men by severing the vas deferens.

VERNIX: a thick, white, oily substance which covers the skin of the fetus.

VERTEX: the crown of the head.

VIABILITY: the capability of living.

Index

Page numbers in bold type indicate illustrations

Abdomen
  striae, 35, 52
  swelling, 30
Abortion
  following surgery, 79
  induced, 79–80
  spontaneous, 24, 50, 59–62
Afterbirth. *See* Placenta
Afterpains, 129–30
Age, effect on pregnancy, 68–69
Alcohol, 46
Alternate birth centers, 5
Amniocentesis
  to detect fetal sex, 53
  to detect genetic defects, 12, 68
  to detect Rh trouble, 73
  fee for, 8
  for induced abortion, 80
  technique, 68–69, **69**
Amniotic fluid, 24, 120
Analgesia, 98–99
Anatomy, female, 16–19, **17**
Anemia
  cause of, 77
  Cooley's, 12
  detection of, 11
  and faintness, 36
  sickle cell, 12
Anesthesia
  caudal, 101–3, **102**, 106
  epidural 101–3, **102**, 106
  fee for, 8
  gas, 100–1, 105, 108
  local, 103, 106
  Pentothal, 101
  spinal, 101–2, **102**, 105–6

Angiomas, 35
Apgar score, 108
Appendicitis, 78

Baby, newborn
  activities, 146, 160
  appearance, 108, 147
  care, 159–61
  circumcision, 148
  clothes and equipment, 151–53
  length, 146
  prediction of sex, 53–54
  premature, 148
  weight, 148
Baby blues, 132
Backache, 34
Bag of waters. *See* Membranes
Baths. *See* Tub baths
Betamethasone, 117
Birth certificate, 150
Birth control, 81, 162–63
Birthing room, 56, 104
Bleeding
  after delivery, 158–59
  with miscarriage, 60
  with placenta previa, 124
  with placental separation, 124
  in pregnancy, 14, 60
Blood pressure
  during pregnancy, 13
  in toxemia, 74
Bloody show, 90–91
Bottle feeding, 144–46
Bowels
  after delivery, 131
  during pregnancy, 34

Brassiere
    after delivery, 131, 143
    during pregnancy, 51
Breast
    care, 52, 143
    engorgement, 130–31, 144, 159
    infection, 133
    shield, 143
    striae, 35, 52
    swelling, 29–30
Breast feeding. *See* Nursing
Breech presentation, 126–27, **126**

Calcium, 11, 32, 43, 52, 158
Calisthenics
    after delivery, 157
    during pregnancy, 48–49
Calories, 42
Carbohydrates, 43
Catheterization
    after delivery, 131
    in labor, 97
Caudal anesthesia, 101–3, **102**,
    106
Cephalopelvic disproportion,
    120–21
Cervix
    anatomy of, 16, **17**
    after delivery, 161
    incompetent, 87
    in labor, 88–89, **88–89**, 90
    in pregnancy, 88–89
Cesarean section, 121–23
    for breech presentation, 127
    fee for, 6, 8
    for placenta previa, 124
    for prematurity, 117
    for slow labor, 119
    and sterilization, 81–82
    for twins, 64
Chromosomes, 19–21, **21**
Cigarettes, 46, 98
Circumcision, 148
Clothes
    for the baby, 151
    in the hospital, 56
    maternity, 51–52
Colostrum, 140
Condom, 163
Congenital deformities. *See*
    Deformities of the fetus
Constipation
    after delivery, 131
    during pregnancy, 34
Contraception. *See* Birth control

Contractions of uterus
    duration, 91, 93
    frequency, 91–92
    intensity, 93–94
    onset, 88
Cord. *See* Umbilical cord
Cramps, leg, 32
Curettage
    after delivery, 158
    for induced abortion, 79
    after spontaneous abortion, 61
Cysts of ovary, 78–79

D and C. *See* Curettage
Danger signs, 14
Deformities of the fetus
    caused by rubella, 65
    relationship to X-rays, 66
    resulting in fetal death, 70
    resulting in miscarriage, 60
    types of deformities, 67–68
Delivery
    breech, 126–27
    by forceps, 106, 113
    at home, 3
    of placenta, 109
    position of patient during, 105
    room, 102–5, **104**
    spontaneous, 106
Demerol, 99
Diabetes, 10, 58–59, 76, 81, 111
Diaphragm, 163
Diet
    after delivery, 157–58
    while nursing, 45, 158
    in pregnancy, 39–46
Discharge, vaginal, 37–38, 47, 159
Disproportion, cephalopelvic, 119
Dizziness, 36, 74
Douching
    after delivery, 156
    after miscarriage, 12, 68–69
    in pregnancy, 46–47
Down's syndrome, 12, 68–69
Drugs
    in labor, 98–99
    in pregnancy, 46
Due date, 84

Eclampsia, 75
Ectopic pregnancies, 22, 62–63, **62**
Egg. *See* Ovum
Elastic stockings, 51
Embryo, **22**
Endometrium, 18

Epidural anesthesia, 101–3, **102,**
  106
Episiotomy
  pain, 130
  performance, 92, 106, 109–10,
   113
  rationale, 109–10
Erythroblastosis, 11, 73–74
Estrogen, 18
Exercise
  after delivery, 157
  in pregnancy, 45, 48–49

Fainting, 36, 63
Fallopian tube. See Tube
Father of the baby. See Husband
Fertilization, 19–20, **20, 22**
Fetus
  activities, 25
  death, 69–70, 75
  growth, 23–24, **26**
  heartbeat, 15, 53, 64, 70, 96
  movements, 31, 70
  nourishment, 24
  sex, 53
  size, 25, **26**
  weight, 25
Fever, 14
Fibroid tumors, 77
Flatulence, 30
Fluoride, 11, 43–45, 158
Follicle, 17–18, **17, 22**
Forceps delivery, 106, 113
Formula for bottle feeding,
  144–45

Gallstones, 78
Garters, 51
Genetic counseling, 12, 60
German measles. See Rubella
Grandmother
  role after delivery, 56, 154–55,
   155
  role in pregnancy, 55
Groin pains, 34–35

Headache
  and spinal anesthesia, 101
  and toxemia, 74
Health insurance, 8
Heartburn, 31
Hemophilia, 12
Hemorrhage
  after delivery, 158–59
  with miscarriage, 60

  with placenta previa, 124
Hemorrhoids, 33–34, 131
Hormones
  in labor, 86–87
  and nausea, 28
  from ovaries, 17–18, 22–23
Hospital
  arrival at, 92
  choice of, 5
  departure from, 151–53
  duration of stay in, 6, 153
  rates, 9
  routines, after delivery, 149–50
  visiting hours of, 149
  what to take to, 56–57
Husband
  after delivery, 154–55
  at delivery, 115
  in labor, 114–15
  at office visits, 13
  in pregnancy, 38, 54–55
Hysterotomy, 79

Implantation of the egg, **22**
Induction of labor, 111–12
Infection
  bladder, 76, 159
  breasts, 133, 159
  kidneys, 59, 76
  uterus, 159
  veins, 133
Influenza vaccinations, 53
Insomnia, 36
Iron, 11, 36, 43, 77, 158
I.U.D. (Intrauterine device), 81,
  162–63

Jaundice of the newborn, 148

Kidney infection, 59, 76
Knee-chest exercise, 161–62

Labor
  causes of onset, 86–87
  contractions, 91–92
  drugs in, 98–99
  dry, 119–20
  duration of, 89–90, 92–93, 119
  false, 86, 91, 118, 119
  induction of, 111–12
  mechanism of, 86–90
  pain, 91–95
  pelvic exams in, 92
  premature, 64, 78, 117–18
  room, 95

signs of onset, 90–91
slow, 118–19
stages of, 89–90
trial of, 121
Lactation. *See* Nursing
Laparoscopic sterilization, 83
Layette, 151–52
Leg cramps, 32
Lethargy, 29
Lightening, 85–86
Lochia, 132

Marijuana, 46
Measles, German. *See* Rubella
Medicaid, 9
Membranes
    artificial rupture of, 96, 111–12, 120
    delivery of, 90
    description of, 24
    premature rupture of, 116–17
    spontaneous rupture of, 87–88, **88**, 91, 116
Menstruation
    normal cycle, 18
    return, after delivery, 158
    return, after miscarriage, 61
Midwives
    certified, 2
    delivery by, 5–6
    examination by, 13
    lay, 2–3
Migration of the egg, 21
Milk
    in diet, 43–44, 52
    production of mother's, 139–43
Miscarriage, 24, 50, 59–62, 79
Molding of the fetal head, **89**, 108
Mongolism. *See* Down's syndrome
Moodiness, 37
Morning sickness, 28
Mortality
    infant, 1–2, 75
    maternal, 1–2, 75, 77–78
Mother
    diseases, 76–77
    mortality, 1–2, 75, 77–78
Moving, 51

Natural childbirth
    description of, 88, 93–94, 112–15
    exercises, 49
Nausea, 11, 28
Nipples

care after delivery, 141
care before delivery, 52
cracked, 141, 143
inverted, 14, 52–53, 138
pigmentation of, 32
Nosebleeds, 35
Nurse
    for the baby, 156
    in labor room, 92, 95
Nursing, 134–44, **135**
    contraceptive effect, 158, 163
    in the delivery room, 108, 139
    diet for, 45
    preparation for, 13–14, 52

Obstetrician
    fees, 7
    general practitioner as, 4
    partnerships, 6–7
    roles of, 2
    selection of, 3
    specialists, 3–4
    types of, 4
    when to call, 14
Office visits
    after delivery, 116
    the first, 10
    frequency of, 12–13
    number of, 8
    subsequent, 13–14
Ovary
    anatomy of, **17**
    cysts of, 78–79
    follicles of, 18
    hormones of, 18
Overdue pregnancies, 85, 111
Ovulation, 18, **22**
Ovum, 17–21, **20**, 23

Packing a bag, 56
Painting, 51
Pap smear, 11
Pediatrician, 4–5, 149
    fee for, 8
Pelvic examinations
    after delivery, 153
    in labor, 92, 96
    in pregnancy, 11, 14, 78
Pelvis
    measurements, 11, 120
    X-rays of, 66, 120–21
Pentothal, 101
Piles. *See* Hemorrhoids
Pill, birth-control, 81, 163
Pitocin